Michael Dorset

An Essay on Defensive War, and a Constitutional Militia

With an account of Queen Elizabeth's arrangements for resisting the projected

invasion in the year 1588: taken from authentic records in the British museum, and

other collections

Michael Dorset

An Essay on Defensive War, and a Constitutional Militia
With an account of Queen Elizabeth's arrangements for resisting the projected invasion in the year 1588: taken from authentic records in the British museum, and other collections

ISBN/EAN: 9783337218140

Printed in Europe, USA, Canada, Australia, Japan

Cover: Foto ©ninafisch / pixelio.de

More available books at **www.hansebooks.com**

AN

ESSAY

ON

DEFENSIVE WAR,

AND A

CONSTITUTIONAL MILITIA;

WITH AN ACCOUNT OF

Queen ELIZABETH's Arrangements for refisting expected Invafion in the Year 1588, taken from authentic Records in the Britifh Museum, and other Collections.

By an OFFICER.

"To the Lieutenants and Gentlemen of Command in your Counties, I require you to take care That the People be well armed, and in readiness upon all Occasions,"

Queen Elizabeth's Speech to both Houses.

PREFACE.

TO roufe the flumbering fpirit of the nation, and awaken its attention to the dangers which furround it, conftitute the defign of this Effay.—Not only the probable chance of an invafion, but even its poffibility fhould be adverted to and guarded againft.—The prevention of mifchief is at all times a wifer plan than feeking remedies for it; and as far as human reafon can extend its forefight amidft the deliriums of ftatesmen, it feems unlikely that any power on earth would venture the rafh attempt

of

of invading this country, when fyftem-
atically prepared for defence.

From men of obfervation, it will be
no unwelcome compliment to hear, that
this work contains nothing new. It has
never wandered amongft the fhadowy
landfcapes of imagination, or philofo-
phized through the magic lanthorn of hy-
pothefis. A concife ftate of an interefting
fubject, referred to immutable principles,
is all its merit. Few perhaps can apply
to their own reflection without finding
the fame principles, often more refined.
But if it poffefs the luck of referring the
reader to the ftores of his own reafon, it
will anfwer the beft purpofe of many a
better book.—Written in a camp, it has
no claims to correctnefs or elegance of
compofition. Other occupations have prevented fubfequent improvements, and for
a time deftroyed all idea of making it
public. The account of Queen Elizabeth's

beth's arrangements have however been fince added, through the affiftance of a diftinguifhed literary character; and this part of the work, at leaft, demands attention. For the reft, I am too doubtful of its merits to hazard a name, even of no importance.

The preffing fituation of affairs calling it forth at the inftant, have prevented my taking advantage of Horace's counfel; therefore in its prefent ftate it is confided to the generofity of a nation, whofe deareft interefts it concerns.

CONTENTS.

Errata.

Page	Line		For	Read
2	5	From the top	natural	national
2	25	do.	refitt	refort
3	22	do.	toils	toil
7	19	do.	of	and
8	7	do.	neutral	natural
16	15	do.	was here turned	was turned
19	1	do.	them	it
35	9	do.	their	thefe
53	4	do.	natural	national
85	8	do.	is	are
108	19	do.	they	there
113	10	do.	in its execution	in execution
114	4	do.	of	and
116	5	do.	would	fhould
117	7	do.	dle to be	
118	8	do.	with the illuftrious dig- nified names	dignified with the illuf- trious names
118	24	do.	prints	points
118	24	do.	he	the
119	13	do.	all	alone
127	19	do.	legiflature	legiflation
132	10	do.	army	array
142	23	do.	even	ever
144	11	do.	from	form
155	22	do.	parade, etiquette	parade-etiquette
161	8	do.	is	in
161	10	do.	perverts	pervert
162	2	do.	ufuage	ufage
163	10	do.	is carried on	is fometimes carried on
174	10	do.	extremeties	extremities
175	14	do.	is not	be not
193	7	do.	conftantly in quarters	conftantly prefent
194	21	do.	natural defence	national defence
196	14	do.	natural ftrength	national ftrength
197	1	do.	contemptable	contemptible
198	6	do.	principles	principle
199	14	do.	thus	then

PRELIMINARY DISCOURSE.
PROSPECT OF INVASION.

CHAP. I.

WHEN the exigencies of a great nation have driven her to feek fecurity inftead of conqueft; when every view of extending her commerce is loft in its protection, when public credit is fhaken to its bafe, and public wealth exifts but in avoiding bankruptcy, then reflection becomes the virtue of neceffity, and fhe looks around for thofe expedients which her fituation requires and her refources furnifh. At war with her colonies, deferted by her allies, and menaced by the moft powerful combination of hoftile neighbours, it is from herfelf alone fhe can derive protection. What-

B ever

ever means of internal defence nature has beftown muft be called into action. Induftry and fcience are the fprings of motion; the mechanic powers which combine and invigorate the vaft bulk of natural defence, and erect an impregnable fortrefs from an inert mafs of wonderful materials. For in vain are thefe furnifhed by the bounteous hand of Providence, if our workmen are unfkilful in their employ, or no architect has traced a defign for the fabric. The hour of danger can fpare few moments to cool reflection, ftill lefs can it digeft its plans to fage maturity. Projects inftantaneoufly conceived, rafhly adopted, and incorrectly executed, are the natural offspring of furprife; confufion fupplants every idea of regular difpofition; and uncertainty, the darknefs of the mind, like that of the univerfe, doubles every danger that actually exifts, and creates new phantoms of its own. But the nation that in time of tranquility prepares for a defcent has little to fear from it; every advance of the invader produces fome defenfive advantage; every inhabitant knows at the inftant where to refift, and how to con-

ftitute

ftitute a part of national ftrength, inftead of being a fharer in national confufion. That thefe obfervations are well founded may be gathered from the unvarying records of a thoufand hiftories, which enable us to anticipate good conduct by referring to the fate of others; and if experience be the common-fenfe of memory, forefight is the prophetic infpiration of wifdom. A nation unarranged cannot refift. Martial exercifes are infufficient without fome general fyftem of employing them. If the whole country armed it cannot be more military than the *Romans* were; and yet they fuffered heavily when invaded by *Hannibal*, merely from not having previoufly adopted fome plan of defence; half their refources were thrown away before they difcovered how to employ the reft. The fmall alarm occafioned in this kingdom by remote ideas of invafion is matter of curious fpeculation; but with whatever avidity the man of obfervation enters on the toils, it will afford the thanklefs harveft of melancholy reflection. Inftead of that folid confidence derived from well concerted plans, frequently

B 2 practifed,

practised, and thence expertly executed, he
will find the nation lulled by abfurdities almoft
too grofs to mention. On the coafts he will
be told that an invafion has been threatened
every year of every war in their own time
and in their fathers, but as it has not yet happened they have given over expecting it.
The inland counties conceive their diftance
from the fea a fufficient protection : fome
reckon upon the numbers who will arm around
them, while others more illiberal, though
hardly more ridiculous, are happy to defpife
the perfonal courage of their enemies, and
really expect a dozen Englifhmen to difmay a
battalion.

Abfurd and painful as this is to recount, it
is but too faithful a portraiture of national
prejudice. No man ftands forth and tells you
he is not alarmed becaufe a fleet inured to
victory protects our coafts, or that the arrangements of the kingdom are fuch that an
army actually landed could not penetrate ; that
forage would be carried off, roads deftroyed, and bridges broken down with fuch expedition

dition in the midſt of an armed peaſantry, that no invader could by any poſſibility exiſt half the time neceſſary to vanquiſh ſuch ob-ſtruſtions.

Such is the language of reaſon, and when-ever it becomes general in England, the 'word *invaſion* may be obliterated from our dictiona-ries. New *Alexanders* may overrun the globe, and every neighbouring ſtate become a prey to conqueſt, while this nation ſhall retain an undiſturbed tranquility amidſt the wreck of empires. When this enviable ſecurity is pointed out as what ſound policy may ſtill procure, there are not many, who, from a candid view of the very altered predicament a few late years have placed us in, can diſcern what cau-ſes had hitherto rendered invaſions impracti-cable, and how far they have now ceaſed to operate. The ſcene, however gloomy, may be inſtructive, and a few lines will review it. His preſent Majeſty aſcended the throne of theſe realms under every poſſible advantage a young and generous prince could wiſh for. His victorious arms were on every ſide rendering

ing him refpectable abroad, and poffeffed of
all the warmeft wifhes of his fubjects, he reign-
ed fecurely in their hearts at home. He faw
himfelf at once the arbitrer of Europe, the fupreme magiftrate of the happieft government,
and the idol of all its inhabitants. He faw his
commerce improved, his territories enlarged,
his fubjects enriched, and the profpect of a
fpeedy advantageous peace to fecure thefe bleffings in undifturbed enjoyment. With what
heart-felt joy might this fcene be expiated on,
and what reluctant language traces its reverfe.
The great, the perpetuated, the fatal error ori-
ginated in falfe notions of regal power, and a
fuppofition that the greatnefs of a king could
exift independent of the wellfare of the fubject.
This was a long exploded opinion, often re-
vived, and as often confuted, but it prefented
advantages too immediate, and profpects too
fpecioufly alluring not to be tenacioufly adhered to when once adopted. Amidft all the
prevalence of paffion, it required great energy
of foul and manly reafoning to diftinguifh between abfolute and real power: yet there is a
very marked diftinction interwoven between

them

them in the nice texture of our matchlefs conftitution, whence they derive such an inverfe relation, that the one can hardly be augmented without proportionably leffening the other. This also is no modern difcovery, fince a great ftatefman long ago obferved, in expreffions too ftrong not to ufe his own language. *Quand un Roi d'Angleterre eſt l'homme de ſon peuple c'eſt le plus grand Roi du monde; véut il etre plus! il n'eſt rien.*

Notwithſtanding the aweful puniſhment and ultimate failure of all encroachments on the nation's rights in earlier days, ſuch attempts were now inceſſantly repeated, and the court revolted into open rebellion againſt the people.

This, however, was not an age in which the iron graſp of power was uſhered with gigantic ſtrides of ſavage countenance. Confifcation and profcription were unknown; juſtice between individuals was fairly adminiſtred; and no private oppreſſions extorted a complaint from injured innocence. The attacks

tacks on the conftitution itfelf were from mafked batteries, and a fecret undermining influence was deftroying that fabric by fap which ten thoufand *Machiavelian* armies would have been repulfed from in attempting to ftorm. The fate of other empires teaches us to expect a period to our political as well as neutral exiftence; and as the ftones on the fea-beach, from conftantly rolling together, acquire a like figure, fo it is probable we are too much affimilated in manners and opinions with the nations round, to be long poffeffed of any fuperiority in the form of government. It is not neceffary here to fpecify the mournful catalogue of events which ftain our annals, or to dwell upon their having arifen from increafe of *influcuce*, the only engine a mild and gracious prince could employ to change a conftitution.

But it muft be obferved that the nation, not entering into the neceffity of alteration and averfe to innovation, however mildly introduced, feemed to recollect that the high rank it held in the fcale of empires was

owing

owing to fomething more than its foil, extent, or fituation, and wifhed to preferve its greatnefs by every advantage that had confpired to raife it; hence this growing influence was watched with jealous eyes, and the extreme unpopularity of their meafures foon occafioned an oftenfible change in the king's firft minifters, and whether the very fame men fecretly continued to prefide, is perfectly immaterial to the public, whofe feelings continued to be outraged, and whofe rights to be violated by the unaltered predominancy of unconftitutional meafures.—Univerfal difcontent occafioned new arrangements, fucceffive adminiftrations were repeatedly formed and difcarded with indecent rapidity : always accelerated by any untractable virtue of their conftituent members. The principles of one man, the integrity of another were infurmountable difqualifications whenever they intruded, and it employed feveral years to pack a compleat miniftry from the dregs of every party ; however the plan was at length moft diabolically effected, and *Lord North* ftood forth the Lucifer of the Pandæmonium.

A pow-

A powerful oppofition raifed againft this junto at home engaging all their attention, the prefervation of themfelves became the firft object of their care; for this purpofe, they went all lengths to fecure the royal countenance, by making common caufe to fcreen proceedings which were feldom right, under the fanction of that power which *can do no wrong*; thus by artfully amalgamating them together, the popularity of the moft beloved fovereign alloyed with the deteftation of his minifters, reduced both almoft below the common currency of daily expenditure; and by fhifting off all refpofibility among themfelves, the public odium became indivifible and fell in the lump: even the private virtues of their mafter were eternally called in to ballance their negative qualities, and fwell their intolerable demands. Revered as thefe virtues were, men prudently obferved, that to entruft a monarch with the power to deftroy, becaufe he had the will to fave, would be like infecting a nation with the plague, becaufe there was a phyfician likely to cure it.

In

In vain then did individuals murmur, and the kingdom at large follow petitions by remonftrances. The parliament which *Bacon* and *Montefquieu* had foreboded as the only certain ruin to this conftitution, was now wholly devoted to the crown, and with a little variance of form held its beds of juftice but to regifter the edicts of the cabinet; fome efpecial ceremonies of ancient days were indeed preferved, for the minority *faid* what they pleafed, as compleatly as the minifters *did it*.—When reafon, ftubborn fact, or public utility are to be furmounted in grave debate, fome fterling argument muft be adduced to preponderate the buoyant fcale; for this the baneful fyftem of corruption (too fuccefsfully employed by the able hands of *Sir Robert Walpole* ever to be totally relinquifhed) offered the deciding authority; it became the mode, the regular official mode of governing, pervading all ranks, and extending over all fects: electors and elected fuffered the fame infection, which like the plague of *Egyptian* darknefs, overfpread the face of the realm; it was the algebraic character that applied to all problems; the uni-

verfal

verfal menftruum of opinion, and had that
other chemical fecret, the philofophers ftone
been joined to it, twice as many deftinies as
ever covered *Troy* could not have preferved
this nation from deftruction. But the higheft
exertions of human ingenuity have their
limits, for bribery itfelf is neither an art or a
fcience, fcarce even what mechanics call a
craft, it is fo obvious to the meaneft capacity
that a baby may perform it as fortunately as
a politician; and if it has been fo fuccefsfully
practifed by Punch at an election, it were an
ill compliment to fuppofe our minifters lefs
dexterous. Ufortunately, however, corruption
although it may claim the attributes of omni-
potence and infallibility, is none of thofe felf-
dependent beings which are co-eval with eter-
nity, and promife an equal duration. Unfortunately, I fay, bribery hath its dependencies,
and when places had been multiplied and honours proftituted, till they even loft their
nature, money was found to be the firft great
caufe, the effence and the foul of modern government. To procure this plentifully from a
nation already overwhelmed with enormous
debts,

feemed beyond the power of this great agent itfelf, which could no longer prey upon its own bowels and be at once effect and caufe.——Hence the cabinet were driven to explore diftant fhores for that golden harveft which an impoverifhed foil too fparingly afforded.——An oppofition, refpectable from its number, from its confequence, and more fo from the characters of thofe who compofed it, was to be contended with ; and money was the artillery to be employed on fuch a fervice.—The lavifh expenditure, compleat mifmanagement, and infamous peculation of the public treafure had almoft annihilated any fuch exiftence, more however was neceffary to be procured, and if poffible without aggravating the feelings of a nation already oppreffed.—Neceffity adds wings to the wickednefs of invention ; and the mad project of obtaining a revenue from *America* became the fruitful mother of our prefent misfortunes. In vain were memory, wifdom and prudence invoked to avert the attempt. Juftice alfo was appealed to, but fhe ruled only the politics of *Utopia* , while expediency fupplanted the very word in minifterial gloffaries.—

The

The colonies petitioned, the patriots harangued, the nation murmured, but the Premier carried every meafure he propofed; thefe too were fuggefted by fuch re-iterated madnefs, fuch extravagance of folly, and fuch a fatality of error, as chance alone could hardly have effected; there appeared to be fome talent, fome faculty of blundering, that muft have exceeded the belief of our anceftors had it been foretold, and will ftagger the faith of pofterity, when recorded. That meafures wickedly adopted were weakly executed might eafily be imagined, but furely fome dæmon muft have fhaken his baneful pinions over the council board, if every thing operated exactly contrary to their intentions. When the minifter ftruck at wealth, national beggary was the refult. His endeavours to divide *America*, united the whole continent. His fhutting up their ports deftroyed half the commerce of *England* and ruined the *Weft Indies.*—His witholding our merchandize eftablifhed new manufactures for themfelves; his reftraining their fifheries, manned their navy; his burning their villages, recruited their army; and his attempt at un-

con-

conditional fubmiffion, promifes to terminate in unlimited independence.

Thefe are the outlines filled by a thoufand minuter parts equally aftonifhing, equally exceeding all other tablatures of hiftoric narrative ; whofe very exiftence like that of our own being can hardly be demonftrated but by the immediate evidence of the fenfes.

From this view of our political fituation, we immediately deduce the war with the Houfe of *Bourbon*, and the confequential ideas of invafion which have given birth to this Effay ; for furely the unravelling that clue which led us into danger, is no unfeafonable enquiry towards extricating us from it.——— If a brave and gallant army have been devoted in *America* , this nation amidft all its diftreffes with grateful pity will commiferate their feelings. The veteran who fees himfelf the guardian of the people's liberties, joys to boaft only thofe fcars acquired in the fervice of his country. How few then are there who, without violence to themfelves, could relinquifh

the

the moſt ſacred ties of ſociety, and arm their hands againſt thoſe very bleſſings, which as Men, and Engliſhmen, they had a right to ſhare.——A variance between duty and inclination was but a bad omen to ſtart with, and an army, impelled with reluctance to the field, where every generous paſſion impeded its career, was not likely to atchieve ſuch uncommon feats as the deſperate exigencies of the miniſter required.—It was not the ſtarving pittance of ſubſiſtence that had heretofore crowned our armies with immortal wreaths; every glorious incitement, evey potent ſtimulus, that actuated our great forefathers was here cut off, nay more, was here turned againſt us.—To overrun a vaſt continent, and combat at once againſt numbers and againſt freedom, was too much even for *Britiſh* troops. —Whilſt our regiments were thus mouldering away, and waſting that matchleſs ſpirit, which muſt have dignified every other enterprize; the troops of *Bourbon* were ſeduouſly training for the long-meditated attack. In proportion as our army dwindled, theirs augmented. The inequality widened every hour,

and

and while *America* is to be the fink of our exertions, muft ftill increafe.

Wrecked on the fame fatal coaft, our navy funk into fimilar inferiority. That navy which for ages had hailed this ifland Emprefs of the Deep, and bound *Neptune*'s brows with the *Britiſh* flag ; whofe feamen were the very foul of audacity and enterprife ; and whofe officers with every martial virtue are not only the firſt in their own line, but excell in talents more admirably well adapted than any other fcience can boaft amongſt its profeffors.—A fad reverfe of fortune exhibited this fleet betrayed by higher powers into the neceffity of unwilling flight. Thoufands of Englifh fubjects, from their windows beheld their own danger in their country's difgrace ; and execrations were liberally beftowed on the marine minifter, who after ruining a fleet by the vileft jobs, had driven from the fervice, the ableft and braveft officers, to whom the nation looked up as moft capable of retrieving its ufurped domain. ——Minifters had been too much occupied with their *American Manies,* and parliamentary

D   cabals

cabals at home, to caſt an obſervant eye on what was going forward abroad. Therefore the firſt Lord of the Admiralty, whenever warned by Oppoſition of foreign armaments, regularly exulted with conſummate confidence in his own management, and repeatedly *pledged himſelf* that our navy ſhould be ſuperior to the Houſe of *Bourbon.*—The pawn was but a ſorry ſtake.—Facts turn out fatally re-verſe.——Yet the ſame miniſter ſtill continues in ſpite of univerſal infamy, and receives the damning contradiction of events with an un-bluſhing countenance.

The Proſpect of *Invaſion* ſtands therefore on very different grounds, from thoſe of the laſt war ; when ſhielded by the powers of an unrivalled navy, *Great Britain* reſted in perfect ſecurity herſelf, while the whole world lay open to her arms. Leſs anxious for her own commerce, than reſolute to cruſh that of her enemies ; the ocean was her own. Not a gale ruffled its boſom, but wafted riches to her merchants, or victory to her flag.—An almoſt undeviating ſeries of ſucceſs had familiariſed

her

her to expect them, and scarce a single sail whitened the horizon of her ports without producing either wealth or conqueft.—Her very bells acquired a monotony of pæans, but then her monarch was a whig, and *Pitt* was minifter.—The fovereign was content to reign by his people's wifhes, and thofe wifhes made him the greateft of monarchs.

Thefe are periods which agonifing memory intrudes upon our feelings. Not to contraft them with the prefent were impoffible; and it is mifery to do fo !———When the great fcale of empires preponderated by the weight of *Britain* ; when the wifdom of her councils begat refpect abroad, and confidence at home ; then commerce increaafed with confequence ; our territories were extended ; our rents rofe; our manufactutes flourifhed ; our merchants were monarchs, and the fovereign himfelf gloried to be diftinguifhed as *the Firft Citizen of the freeft State.*

CHAP.

Hiftoric View of the Principles of Defenfive War.

———————————

A NECESSITY of preparing fome general plan to repel invafion cannot be too often inculcated.—Like the *Delenda eft Carthago* of the Roman Patriot, it fhould preface every page, and terminate every period. Without this, armies will in vain be difciplined, and treafures lavifhed. The nation, who in the hour of fecurity procraftinates the tafk of prudence, will find the moment of danger ill adapted to imbibe inftruction. — From the phyfician who has his art to learn in the crifis of difeafe, the patient will fcarce derive convalefcence.

To

To point out the minute arrangements founded on the *forte* or *foible* of particular diſtricts, would be unwiſe in moſt inſtances, and impoſſible in many. Theſe muſt be the progeny of events; but the grand outlines of all defenſive war, contain no ſecrets for men of military obſervation.

To prevent an enemy actually on our coaſts from effecting a landing, ſeems in theſe times but an hopeleſs chance, if *Britain's* navy is no longer able to protect her there. However, what our intrepid anceſtors have ſucceſsfully practiſed upon *Cæſar* himſelf, may at leaſt excite the imitation of their poſterity. Nor ſhould it be idly urged, that thoſe days of enthuſiaſtic freedom are no more, or that the form of a ſpruce enſign poſſeſſes none of the ſtern virtues which ſteeled the naked boſom of a *Pict*, and led him with brave defiance into the ocean itſelf to meet thoſe boaſted legions, formidable in diſcipline, and glowing with all the pride of conqueſt.—True it is, the poliſhed manners of this age wear a leſs rugged garb, but the gallantry of a Britiſh Soldier remains
unſhaken.

unfhaken.—His foul confides in the fame he-
roic principle. The fame fpark glows in his
breaft, and its emanations are reciprocally
darted through the ranks of a battalion.——
The celeftial flame which beams on the altar
of liberty has at times been latent—half an
age, but has never failed to blaze with undi-
minifhed luftre, when events have called it
forth.—Unextinguifhed through all the viciffi-
tudes of time; bigottry, fanaticifm, oppreffion
and luxury, have in vain attempted its
deftruction; even corruption, more baleful
than them all, has failed in reiterated endeavours to fubdue it.—To this hour it pervades
the multitude, and we have no Romans now
to contend with.—The prefent enemies of
Britain poffefs no invincibility of difcipline
beyond ourfelves; no fuperiority of arms
which we are deftitute of; no warlike engines
tremendous in their effects, and doubly fo by
their novelty. But the conflict becomes really
unequal when we confider the immenfe advantages poffeffed by ourfelves. Moft of thefe
applying to military operations muft be referved for another place. But the different

fprings

fprings of action which operate upon the human mind are] of philofophic confideration and by no means to be difregarded. Thefe controul the orbits of the paffions, roufe them to fly off in excentric tangents, or impel their gravitation towards reafon.—Armies are compofed of individuals whofe diftinct fenfations become the aggregate foul of an expedition. —Let us generoufly attribute to an enemy the nobleft motives, the love of glory and of conqueft; principles too refined to animate the breaft of every private foldier but in a faint degree; their objects are too remote for any permanent impreffion: of the firft his fhare is the indivifible fraction of an idea, from the latter he rarely derives any advantage whatever; fince thofe days are paft when nations fwarmed to feek a more aufpicious home, and every feudatory claiming his portion of glebe conquered for himfelf.

But let fame be their purfuit with all a general's ardour, no Englifhman will allow his country an inferior impulfe, and if we are equal hitherto, what refources remain in ftore! Our

Our liberties, our laws, our religion, our very being itfelf, will make that man an hero, who on minor occafions had been only not a coward. Thefe are fenfations within the reach of every one. Thefe offer to our fenfes, tangible fubftantial good, and will rouze the honeft citizen, who, with unfeduced admiration, had fuffered glory to pafs on, fmiling at the unreal advantage of her gilded vifions.

If the fond partner of a man's happier days fhould look up to a hufband's arm for protection from foreign luft, with mifery in her eye and anguifh in her heart, where is he who would not brave a legion to defend her. If parental affection is doomed to ftream over the mangled bodies of his infants, or to find them in the laft agonies ftretching out their little arms to embrace a father, who comes too late for any thing but torture; tell me, ye who read the human foul, will this man fly in the engagement of to-morrow?—If an helplefs parent, a fick friend, a beloved maiden remain a prey to cruelty in fome deferted village, will no feelings urge to vindicate

their

their wrongs? Shall we fee our houfehold gods themfelves, with the venerable manfions of our anceftors devoted to the flames, without kindling as they burn?—No, my countrymen, we fhall arm ourfelves on fome facred fpot, which with the birthright of liberty has been received from our forefathers; acquired by their virtue, it fhall be maintained by ours, and with every hallowed privilege be tranfmitted to pofterity.—There, environed by our deareft connexions, ftimulated by love, duty, gratitude and juftice, each village will be invincible to armies. Our laws and liberties depend on us and will be gallantly fupported. Nay, there are fortreffes confecrated by enthufiaftic freedom to an impregnability beyond the adamantine walls of magic ftory. *Britons* might unite in Runneymede and brave the univerfe.

An energetic confidence thus built upon the nobleft foundation, removes all anxiety for the ultimate event of an invafion. No one dreams of *Norman conquefts,* or permanent fubjection; but to diminifh the immediate

E   mifchief,

mifchief, to fave our towns from being facked, our villages from being laid wafte, and our country from depopulation, are objects of no trifling importance.——All evils are better prevented than remedied ; and this ifland cannot fupport that procraftination of defence, which a continent like *America* fubmits to without ruin.—The fyftem is the fame, but on a different fcale. The wealth, the cultivation, the conftitution itfelf, all offer infurmountable objections againft permitting extenfive inroads. Hazarding an engagement to prevent them, is, of all expedients, the moft dangerous, and fortified places do not exift. —Multiplied obftructions are the only refource; and thefe are fo abundantly fufficient, that an enemy, who unmolefted could almoft threaten the capital in two days, might by them be effectually reftrained from penetrating in any part above thirty miles from his own fleet.

Having obferved that the internal parts of this ifland afford no fortifications to retard the progrefs of an enemy, the neceffity of checking him by an engagement will obtrude itfelf

upon

upon many, as it has too generally done during the late encampments. But every reasoning principle and all the authorities of history unite to combat so fatal an error.

Whatever is most essential to the invader, the inhabitants ought studiously to avoid. This is a *postulatum* which will readily be granted, and it will appear that to encounter the army of the country, must be the first object of every grand invasion, for the partial inroads of buccaneering parties, or flying squadrons, have merely plunder and depredation in view instead of conquest. Nor could these have any possibility of existence, if every maritime country were once associated for its own defence, in the manner hereafter to be pointed out.

So long as the army of the country remains opposed to the invader, he can make no movements either with safety or effect. A line of posts lengthening as he advances must be preserved to secure a retreat whilst there remains a chance of being defeated. Forage will

E 2   be,

be, with difficulty, if at all, procured, and his army conſtantly harraſſed in a manner that muſt alone deſtroy it. But the oppoſing force once routed, all theſe diſadvantages vaniſh. He becomes maſter of the country ; reconnoitres at eaſe its inmoſt receſſes; choice guides his marches, which before were governed by neceſſity, and his troops in unmoleſted confidence penetrate further in one day, than a month of inceſſant ſtruggles could have effected before. In ſhort, it is an inconteſtible fact, that an invader who defeats the army of the country never fails to accompliſh his purpoſe thereby ; unleſs its object be remote enough to furniſh leiſure for aſſembling other levies conducted on wiſer principles.

Hiſtory is the ſureſt parent of juſt deciſion. Her leſſons are equally devoid of wild hypotheſis or vulgar error. To argue on what is to come, from that which has conſtantly happened, is preferable to the ſallies of fantaſtic imagination or the learned perplexities of refined theory ; and when the ſoundeſt principles of reaſon apply to cauſes which have invariably

bly p᾽ ᴗᴗᴗced the fame effects, they may fall
fhort of mathematical demonftration, but will
fcarce imprefs lefs conviction.   The inftances
thus furnifhed by memory are too numerous
and too pointed tᴖ be filently paffed over:
leifure and the affit᷄ance of a library might
have improved the felection.

The important rank which *Carthage* formerly held in the fcale of empires, and her con-
nections with *Rome*, have attracted the attention of the moft able hiftorians, and alone
afford the ampleft harveft of experience, without tracing her through the various petty
inroads of *African* powers, tho᾽ ᷄ great invafions
in which fhe bore a fhare and which have been fo
faithfully related fhall be the object of a fhort
difcuffion.——*Agathocles* forefeeing advantages
to be derived from making *Carthage* the feat
of war, while their forces were occupied in the
fiege of his own capital, for the fafety of which
he was under no apprehenfions ; embarked in
perfon for the coaft of *Africa*, where fo unex-
pected a vifitor fpread immediate confterna-
tion.——*Carthage* however in the midft of
commerce

commerce was too opulent not to furnish another army with great expedition. The modes of raising troops are in all countries objects of daily practice, and the presence of an enemy only expedited their success; for whenever plans are actually arranged, danger always promotes rapidity, and calls forth exertions. It seemed a prosperous omen that the levies thus raised, were at once sent out superior to the invader, thus far however the state of *Carthage* had only been executing in war what it had been accustomed to in peace, and left no opening either for confusion or error; but as the system of resisting invasions had never been deliberated on, it was not probable that this army should at once adopt the proper line of conduct; it therefore listened to the first impulse, fought a battle immediately, and being defeated, left the enemy master of the country with all its advantages, which soon led him to the gate of their capital. Without entering into the detail of operations it is sufficient to observe, that repeated defeats and a total defect of system exposed the *Carthaginians* to all the ravages of the conqueror, nor was it till

the

the fourth year of the war that they discovered
their error, and adopted such plans as could
not have failed of succeeding on the very first
landing of *Agathocles*, as compleatly as they
did the moment they were put in practice;
for at length the Senate of *Carthage*, compelled
to wisdom, divided their forces into three
bodies, and after defeating some detachments
sent against them by the son of *Agathocles*, they
blocked him up near *Tunis*; and the historian
precisely says all the passes and roads were
secured to the distance of an hundred furlongs,
whereby all supplies of provisions were entirely cut off, and the invaders reduced to the
certain defeat which famine must have atchieved : thus without hazard to themselves, this
salutary measure at once changed the face of
the war, and he who had been conqueror in an
hundred battles, saw himself at once vanquished
by the grave deliberations of a council, without a blow being struck. An example like
this is not to be neglected ; it enforces beyond
the logic of ten thousand arguments. The
sequel of the history follows naturally. *Agathocles* himself arrived at the instant, he had

hopes

hopes that an enemy whofe want of fyftem he had long taken advantage of, were not grown compleatly wife, and endeavoured to entice them to a battle as heretofore ; but the influence of madnefs and folly was paft : the engagement was refufed ; and *Agathocles*, compelled to attack their entrenchments, was repulfed, his army mutinied, and at length furrendered. Himfelf after being put in irons, efcaped under cover of darknefs and confufion.

The fituation and conduct of the *Romans* in the fecond *Punick* war is a recorded leffon of the higheft authority. Their fubfequent conduct proves them to have been at firft furprifed without a fyftem. They hazarded battles and were defeated. *Hannibal* acquired allies with victories ; and thus inftead of being fubject to the inconveniencies attending an invader, he poffeffed every requifite to carry on the war on equal Terms. The *Romans* trembling for the very feat of empire, imputed their difafters to want of generalfhip in their commanders, nor was it till after their defeat

at

at *Thrasymene*, that they difcovered their proceeding from want of fyftem in themfelves.
From this period, the appointment and conduct of *Fabius* changed the face of the war
during his command, but the battle of *Cannæ*
loft by his fucceffor again plunged his country
into the extreme of mifery, and held forth to
pofterity a warning which all their hiftorians
have dwelt upon, and which, but for *Hannibal*'s
mifconduct giving time to reftore the command to *Fabius*, had probably terminated in
the deftruction of the *Roman* greatnefs.

When *Alexander* entered the dominions of
Perfia, one would think he depended on the
natural character of his antagonifts, and even
that his taking with him a much fmaller army
than he might have done, was from a prudential forefight of the hazards incurred from
numbers.—As long as conqueft attended him
all would go well, and on any reverfe, a few
could extricate themfelves with the leaft en-
cumbrance, and were not fo eafily ftarved,
which was the greateft danger. The pupil of
Ariftotle carried too much philofophy into the

F   field,

field, to fufpect a want of it in his cabinet;
and if the council of *Memnon the Rhodian* had
been followed, pofterity might have contem-
plated the retreat of *Alexander* with as much
admiration as ever his conquefts afforded.—
Memnon (fay the hiftorians) endeavoured by
all poffible means to diffuade the fatraps from
giving battle, and advifed them rather to fpoil
and ravage the country, even trampling under
their horfes feet what forage they could not
carry off. The *Perfian* pride revolted at the
idea. *Diodorus Siculus* fays they efteemed it
difhonourable, and cafting a ftain upon their
valour; and for this punctilio rejected the
certainty of fuccefs : the fequel proved that to
conquer the *Macedonians* was no eafy tafk, but
whoever looks at *Darius's* numbers will allow
it to have been perfectly eafy to eat them up.
—National pride of all human ridicule is the
moft ridiculous; it feems a twig of every man's
abfurdity bound into a ftate-faggot. *Zim-
merman* tells us the decent morality of an
elder in an humped-backed nation reftraining the jeers of his countrymen at a perfon
perfectly ftrait, who had been fhipwrecked
amongft

amongſt them, and adviſing rather to go
into the temples to return the Gods thanks
for having endowed themſelves with ſuch
ornamental humps, than to triumph over
the unhappy foreigner who was denied ſuch
a bleſſing.——For individuals, honour eſta-
bliſhes a court of equity, to regulate what law
cannot reach, they become members of ſociety
upon their terms, and whoever embraces an
order is bound to abide by its rules, as long
as he claims its benefits. This legiſlation
like every other has its rewards and puniſh-
ments, not leſs effective for being incoporeal.
Theſe however will only apply to the members of a ſtate, and not to the ſtate itſelf; for
which, opinion has no ſupremacy, but every
thing muſt be ſubſtantiated, there is no ſociety
of empires to claſh or mingle with each other,
no compliment, no preference to virtue, no
reproach for vice, it is the intercourſe between dependent beings, that alone gives influence to ideas; a *Robinſon Cruſce* never once
cared what the world thought of him.—An
individual through exceſs of virtue renounces
like *Helvetius,* an accumulating fortune, and

F 2   we

we revere his difintereftednefs; but let a nation fcrutinize the right of conqueft aud relinquifh a valuable territory acquired by their anceftors, will the fame morality apply, and enfure the confcientious monarch fimilar applaufe? If it be allowed meritorious to facrifice our interefts in the one cafe, and neceffary always to purfue them in the other, does it not follow that this vapour of common life, this aërial code of opinion extends an impotent jurifdiction beyond our private actions? We hear of national difgrace, what is it? who feels, who owns it? does it leffen the dignity of a city-knight, interfere with the confequence of a country juftice, or deftroy the importance of a great man's butler? do you, or any of your friends, find yourfelves one atom more mean and contemptible for your fhare of difgrace? Can you put a nation out of countenance, pull it by the nofe, or fet it in the pillory? for in good truth unlefs you can fubftantiate evil, the honeft citizen who feels his commerce improving and his taxes eafy, will not take the trouble of being convinced how much his country is difgraced by

the

the conceſſions which procured him theſe advantages.—On the other hand, national honour
is either ſo indiviſible that no-body gets a
ſhare of it, or its corpuſcles are too minute
even for microſcopic obſervation. We are
fond enough of diſplaying our glories in general, and yet none that I know have aſked
any credit upon the authority of being ſtock-
holders in this general fund. The dunce in
his pulpit, the clerk in his ſtave, the fox-hunter at his leap, and the merry andrew in his
grin, are each fond enough of honour to expect it in their line, but they only claim what
is due to their private merits. The abuſe of
language has produced more confuſion than any
perverſion of intellect ever did ; in borrowing
a word to which ideas have once been rightly
applied, we bear off all thoſe ideas to ſome
topic which they cannot fit ; but becauſe we
find a coat commodious in private life, ſhall
we freight a cargo of cloathing for an unin-
habited iſland. If national honour be then
only a word without meaning, it were to be
wiſhed it had been explained before we had
ſo much diſpute about it with the *Americans.*

any

Any thing but unconditional fubmiffion would affect the honour of this country, by and bye this country's honour may talk of unconditional fubmiffion with the trifling difference of having it change fides. We debate wifely about acknowledging their independence, when perhaps it might not be amifs to get them to guarantee our own.

When *Charles* V. invaded *France,* her monarch was too wife to overlook the decifive mode of fruftrating his ambition, and the reafonablenefs of his conduct was diftinguifhed by fuch marked features that no able hiftorian however unacquainted with military affairs, could fail remarking them. *Francis* (fays *Robertfon*) fixed upon the only proper and effectual plan for defeating the invafion of a powerful enemy, and his prudence in chufing this plan, as well as his perfeverance in executing it deferve the greater praife as it was equally contrary to his own natural temper, and the genius of the *French* nation, he determined to remain altogether upon the defenfive, never to hazard a battle, or even a great fkirmifh, without certainty

tainty of fuccefs ; to fortify his camps in a
regular manner ; to throw garrifons only into
towns of great ftrength ; to deprive the enemy of fubfiftence by laying wafte the country
before them, and to fave the whole kingdom
by facrificing one of its provinces.——The
execution of this plan, he committed entirely
to the Marechal *Montmorency*, who was the
author of it ; a man wonderfully fitted by nature for fuch a truft, haughty, fevere, confi-
dent in his own abilities, and defpifing thofe
of other men, incapable of being diverted from
any refolution by remonftrances or entreaties,
and in profecuting any fcheme regardlefs alike
of love and of pity.

Montmorency made choice of a ftrong camp
under the walls of *Avignon*, at the confluence
of the *Rhone* and the *Durance*, one of which
plentifully fupplied his troops with all neceffaries from the inland provinces, and the
other covered his camp on that fide where it
was moft probable the enemy would approach ;
he laboured with unwearied induftry to render
the fortifications of this camp impregnable,

and

and affembled there a confiderable army, though greatly inferior to that of the enemy, while the king with another body of troops encamped at *Valence* higher up the *Rhone*. *Marfeilles* and *Arles* were the only towns he thought neceffary to defend, the former in order to retain the command of the fea, the latter as the barrier of the province of *Languedoc*, and each of thefe he furnifhed with numerous garrifons of his beft troops commanded by officers, on whofe fidelity and valour he could rely. The inhabitants of the other towns, as well as of the open country were compelled to abandon their houfes, and were conducted to the mountains, to the camp at Avignon or the inland provinces. The fortifications of fuch places as might have afforded fhelter or defence to the enemy, were thrown down. Corn, forage, and provifions of every kind were carried away or deftroyed; all the mills and ovens were ruined ard the wells filled up or rendered ufelefs. The devaftation continued from the *Alps* to *Marfeilles*, and from the fea to the confines of *Dauphine*, nor does hiftory afford any inftance among civilized nations, in which

this

this cruel expedient for the public fafety was employed with the fame rigour. Meanwhile the emperor arrived with the van of his army on the frontiers of *Provence*, and was ftill fo poffeffed with confidence of fuccefs, that during a few days when he was obliged to halt until the reft of his troops came up, he began to divide his future conquefts among his officers, and, as a new incitement to ferve him with zeal, gave them liberal promifes of offices, lands, and honours in *France*. The face of defolation however, which prefented itfelf to him when he entered the country, began to damp his hopes, and convinced him that a monarch, who, in order to diftrefs an enemy, had voluntarily ruined one of his richeft provinces, would defend the reft with obftinate defpair. Nor was it long before he became fenfible that *Francis*'s plan of defence was as prudent, as it appeared to be extraordinary. His fleet, on which *Charles* chiefly depended for fubfiftence, was prevented for fome time by contrary winds, and other accidents to which naval operations are fubject, from approaching the French coaft; even after its arrival, it afforded

at

at beſt a precarious and ſcanty ſupply to ſuch
a numerous body of troops; nothing was to
be found in the country itſelf for their ſup-
port, nor could they draw any conſiderable aid
from the dominions of the Duke of *Savoy*, ex-
hauſted already by maintaining two great armies. The Emperor was no leſs embarraſſed
how to employ, than how to ſubſiſt his forces,
for though he was now in poſſeſſion of almoſt
an entire province, he could not be ſaid to
have the command of it while he held only
defenceleſs towns, and while the French, beſides their camp at *Avignon*, continued Maſters
of *Marſeilles* and *Arles*.—At firſt he thought
of attacking the camp, and of terminating the
war by one deciſive blow, but ſkilful officers,
who were appointed to view it, declared the
attempt to be utterly impracticable; he then
gave orders to inveſt *Marſeilles* and *Arles*,
hoping that the French would quit their advantageous poſts in order to relieve them:
but *Moutmorency*, adhering firmly to his plan,
remained immoveable at *Avignon*, and the Im-
perialiſts met with ſuch a warm reception from
the garriſons of both towns, that they relin-
quiſhed

quished their enterprizes with lofs and difgrace.
As a laft effort, the Emperor advanced once
more towards *Avignon*, though with an army
harraffed by the perpetual incurfions of fmall
parties of the French light troops, weakened
by difeafes and difpirited by difafters which
feemed more intolerable, as they were unex-
pected.

The hiftorian, in the next fection, recites
the dangers to which *Montmorency* was expofed
by the ardour of his own army, and that of
Francis, who arrived to take the command,
and was touched with their difcontent at this
appearance of timidity, when he continues.—
Happily the retreat of the enemy delivered
the kingdom from the danger which any rafh
refolution might have occafioned. The Emperor after fpending two inglorious months
in *Provence*, without having performed any
thing fuitable to his vaft preparations, or that
could juftify the confidence with which he had
boafted his own power, found that, befides
Antonio de Leyva and other officers of diftinction, he had loft one half of his troops by

difeafes

difeafes or by famine, and that the reft were
in no condition to ftruggle any longer with
calamities, by which fo many of their compa-
nions had perifhed. Neceffity therefore extorted from him orders to retire ; and though
he was fometime in motion before the French
fufpected his intention, a body of light troops,
affifted by crouds of peafants eager to be re-
venged on thofe who had brought fuch deftruction on their country, hung upon the
rear of the Imperialifts, and by feizing every
opportunity of attacking them, threw them
often into confufion. The road by which they
fled, (for they purfued their march with fuch
diforder and precipitation, that it hardly de-
ferves the name of a retreat,) was ftrewed with
arms or baggage, which in their hurry and
trepidation, they had abandoned, and covered
with the fick, the wounded, and the dead ; in-
fomuch that *Martin Bellay*, an eye-witnefs of
their calamities, endeavours to give his readers
fome idea of it, by comparing their miferies
to thofe which the Jews fuffered from the
victorious and deftructive arms of the Romans,
if *Montmorency* at this critical moment had
come

come up with all his forces, nothing could have saved the whole Imperial army from utter ruin. But that General, by ftanding fo long and fo obftinately on the defenfive, had become cautious to excefs; his mind, tenacious of any bent it had once taken could not affume a contrary one as fuddenly as the change of circumftances required; and he ftill continued to repeat his favorite maxims that it was more prudent to allow the lion to efcape, than to drive him to defpair, and that a bridge of gold fhould be made for a retreating enemy.

The prefent moment prefents us with a ftriking feature in the outline of defenfive war, but the fubject is tender; and no man chufes to comment upon a period concerning which the feelings of his readers are fo " tremblingly alive."—Not to extoll much of the *Americans* conduct would be making a public default in the account of juftice; and the author whofe ardent prayer is for the welfare of *Great Britain* gladly relinquifhes the theme, however appofite to his defign.

CHAP.

CHAP. III.

Internal Arrangements of England *in former Periods.*

THE Military Tenures placed our anceſtors in a much more advantageous poſture of defence at all times, than the militia alone can afford to ourſelves. Not only on account of the actual numbers bound to immediate ſervice, but from that univerſal habitude to arms, which conſecrated the exerciſes of every peaſant to the hallowed object of his country's ſafety.—Notwithſtanding theſe feudal advantages, an equal prevalence of military enterpriſes in ſurrounding nations, rendered the interpoſition of the legiſlature frequently neceſſary for the purpoſes of regulating and arraying the ſoldiers thus raiſed; as well as

eſtabliſheftablifhing general and ftated provifions of armour' for the public defence. Accordingly all our old records are full of fuch regulations. There is in the Mufeum, a writ of *Ed.* II. giving to *John,* Earl of *Suffex,* the cuftody of the fea-coafts, and commanding him to array *all* the men between 16 and 60 years of age, for its defence. To the Archbifhop of *Canterbury* and other bifhops is given a power of adminiftering the facrament, to exact from the faid earl and others (called *Cuftodes Portarum*) a folemn oath of fidelity, that the ports allotted to their charge be diligently kept, and alfo that they fhall infpect and fee that all the men of all the counties in *England,* be provided with proper arms fuitable to their condition *.——— At this time the coafts and even the whole kingdom were formed into diftricts, and the charge of each given to particular perfons, fome of thefe diftributions are yet preferved, and their extent feems very

---

* *Juxta ftatum fuum* is the old law expreffion, and there are ftatutes expreffing the fize, weight, and nature of weapons, to be furnifhed by particular qualifications of eftate.

{mall

ſmall.' It appears alſo, that the diviſions of counties and hundreds were originally adopted as well for defenſive as civil purpoſes. For the Mirror ſays, " When kings were firſt or-
" dained in this realm, the kingdom was di-
" vided into forty portions, and every one of
" thoſe portions or counties was * committed
" to ſome earl to govern and defend againſt
" the enemies of the realm. Theſe earls after
" they had received the government of each
" county, divided them into centuries or hun-
" dreds, to every hundred was appointed a
" centurion or conſtable, who had his portion
" and limits aſſigned to him to keep and
" defend with the power of the hundred, and
" were to be ready on all alarms with their
" arms againſt the common enemy."

In the warlike reign of *Edward* III. mili-
tary arrangements are without number, I have annexed a few in the Appendix, ſhewing his

* Formerly the lieutenants of every county were elected by the freeholders (See *Lambard's Saxon Law,*) There was a tract publiſhed in 1642, impeaching the validity of the militia ordinances on this ground.

universal

univerſal array of all lay-men between 16 and
60, as well knights and eſquires, as others capable of bearing arms, under the ſevereſt penalties of life and limb and univerſal forfeiture.
Alſo his charge of the beacons, which were no
new eſtabliſhment, and allowance of procuring
ſubſtitutes in ſome inſtances.————Without
ſwelling the appendix with an unneceſſary
number of authorities, it may be ſufficient to
obſerve, that this array was only for the purpoſe of defenſive war; in which caſe alone it
could be juſtified, and that the calling out
the whole body with ſome exceptions, when
only a few were to be actually employed, was
in fact no more than happens with us, when
freſh ballots are demanded for the militia;
except as to the article of all being furniſhed
with arms, the reaſon of which difference will
appear the moment we recollect the accoutre-
ments with which a ſoldier then entered the
field, and that his armour muſt have been
adapted to his own perſon; whereas now a
muſket at once fits the ſhoulder of a ſubſtitute, as well as that of his principal.————
In the courſe of this eſſay, it has been ob-

H   ſerved,

ferved, that the powers of being ufeful in defence extended to many who were ill-adapted to the bufinefs of attack, or more active operations of a campaign, and there is a paffage too ftrongly worded in the orders fent the Mayor of *Lynn*, for me not to conceive it conveyed the fame meaning. The inftructions for array in this inftance being not of all able men, but it is expreffed to be on the alarm of invafion, and therefore all men capable of defence *(omnes bomines defenfibiles)* are to be called upon.——After muftering the whole numbers of the realm, we have an account of thofe actually ordered to be embodied; and although fome of the counties are miffing, and the quota to be furnifhed by the cities not fully afcertained; they amount to upwards of feventy thoufand, who during the time the king remained in *Scotland*, were affembled in two bodies, at *London* and at *Norwich*, under different commanders, with a ftrong exhortation to orderly demeanour, which the turbulence of the age rendered neceffary.——Befides thofe who by their tenures were bound to maintain particular diftricts, we find frequent inftances of writs for fuch

feryice,

service. The original of one of these is preserved in the Museum, it is in Henry VIths
time, commanding divers persons of the county
of *Dorset, to make watch and ward, and keep the
town and port of the Pool, and coasts of the sea
thereabout,* concluding—*These be the names of
the persons that be bounden to keepe watch and
warde.*—a great many of these names are still
legible, and there can be no doubt but that
whenever it becomes necessary to make serious
provision for defence at home, we shall revert
to the wisdom of our ancestors, and specify the
nature of the aid required from every individual. There are periods of antiquity, to which
the arts look up with gratitude and veneration,
here the senses all conspire against our arro-
gance, and compel us to yield the palm, but
in matters of philosophy and all abstract spe-
culations, being fortunately preserved from the
humiliation of such palpable inferiority, we
avenge ourselves by assuming the haughtiest
pre-eminence; thus as if truth, changed with
the fashions of the court, antiquated knowledge
becomes a term of ridicule. May it not be

H 2   that

that we fee ourfelves do worfe, and only fancy we reafon better ?

Whoever relates the tranfanctions of former ages, of courfe muft borow all he writes. So long as fidelity guides his narration, he can add nothing of his own but fuch remarks as arife from the nature of the fubject, either tending to elucidate the facts themfelves, or to draw conclufions from them. It will therefore, be allowable, to ufe the very words of *Stowe* and *Camden,* in referring to the fituation of this country under *Queen Elizabeth:* with a view of proving that a fovereign, whom heaven had endowed with thofe tranfcendent faculties of difcernment requifite to felect an able miniftry, could never leave this ifland unprepared, when an invafion was meditated. The neceffity of forming previous arrangements for general defence, was in itfelf a difcovery, which like thofe of *Columbus,* left all that was to follow any eafy tafk. Unfortunately, the geographical allufion may be purfued to a refemblance with what old maps reprefented *Van Diemen's Land;* a point hit

upon

upon by our forefathers, which their children long again loft fight of. The Refolution therefore, of timely calling forth, combining and methodizing the powers of natural defence, was fuch an advanced ftage on the road to wifdom, as opened every profpect of the whole career; and if hiftory had been wholly filent upon the fubfequent proceedings, it would have been Cynically uncandid, not to have augured well for them. When a fun beams forth, it muft illumine an hemifphere; and no man who views the ftupendous foundation of an *Egyptian* pyramid, could conceive it intended to fupport a pidgeon-houfe. To argue merely *a priori* it was impoffible for fuch a council, ftarting from fuch a point not to have adopted proper meafures. Hiftorians have fortunately furnifhed us with the means of remarking, that they actually did refolve on the moft wife, the moft falutary, and the only ones certain of attaining their object. Meafures backed by all the experience of remote ages, enforced by all the invincibility of found reafoning, and approved by every eftablifhed principle of military fcience.

ence. It was not the fenfelefs pageantry of review camps, ufelefs but to entertain idlers, at COMPIEGNE*, and harrafs a difgufted army with an unvaried repitition of trifling manœuvres; but one great, rational, well-digefted plan, produced in full maturity by the energy of manly councils, and moft heartily adopted by a free and united people, whofe confidence in government, and approbation of its meafures, mutually begot and foftered each other. *Stowe* begins with remarking the queen's "*pro-*
"*vident regard of her own, her peoples, and coun-*
"*try's fafety*" and *her fubjeƐts exceeding forward-*
nefs in their juft defence, which was promoted for two years together by every method the council could fuggeft, caufing he fays, *the minifters to manifeft to their congregation, the furious purpofe of the Spanifh King, &c.* " by
" whofe pains and induftrie, the *Englifh* na-
" tion were fo combined in heart, that I here
" confeffe I want art lively to expreffe the
" fympathy of love betweene the fubjeƐts and the foveraigne.

* Where the King of *France* ufually has his Review Camps.

" Citties

" Citties, counties, towns, and villages, the
cinque ports, and all other havens of *England*,
manifested as great forwardnes in their zealous
love and dutie, as 'eyther subjects coulde per-
" forme, or prince expect. To single out
" the admirable dexterity and bountie of any
" one perticular place, or people, were ap-
" parent wrong to all, yet for a taste, of
" truth, in all thus much may be sayde of
" *London:* After the counsell had demanded
" what the cittie would doe in their prince
" and countries right, the lord maior and
" aldermen humblie besought their honors to
" sette downe what their wisdomes held re-
" quisite in such a case. The lords demand-
" ed five thousand men and fifteen ships;
" the cittie craved two days respite for an-
" swere, which was granted; and then en-
" treated their lordships, in signe of their per-
" fect love and loyaltie to their prince and
countrey, kindly to accept tenne thousand
" men, and thirtie shippes amply furnished;
" and even as *London*, *London*-like, gave the
" president, the whole kingdom kept true
" rank and equipage.

" The

" The whole nobilitie, moft nobely, like
" planets of the higher orbes, in kind con-
" junction knit their harts in one whofe
" princely valour equalling their love, af-
" fured their foveraygne of triumphant vic-
" torie.

" About three yeares before, at which
" time the Cittie of *London* was greatly trou-
" bled and charged with continuall mufters
" and trayning of foldiers; certaine gallant
" and active citizens, having had experience
" both abroad and at home, voluntarily ex-
" ercifed themfelves, and trayned uppe others
" for the readie ufe of warre, fo as within
" two yeares there was almoft three hundred
" marchants, and others of like quality, very
" fufficient to traine and teach common foul-
" diers the managing their pieces, pikes, and
" halberds, to march counter-march, and
" ring, which faid marchants for their owne
" perfection in military affayres and difci-
" pline, met every Tuefday in the yeare,
" practifing all ufuall poyntes of warre, every
" man by turne bare orderly office, from the
" corporall

" corporall to the captaine, fome of them this
" yeare had charge of men in the great camp,
" and were generally called Captaines of the
" Artillerie Garden, and thefe tooke prefident
" from the merchants of Antwerp." After
mentioning fome naval arrangements, which
have no immediate reference to thefe times,
he proceeds

" Thus the queen having fent competent
" centinells and ftrength to guard her confines,
" and fecure her lands from fudden invafion :
" the counfel upon mature deliberation gave
" order for the executing and difpofing the
" land fervice, and chiefly what ftrength and
" in what place were beft to plant to the armie
" of defence, and in the end it was concluded
" the rendevous fhoulde be at *Tilbury*. The
" ground having been furveyed before, forth-
" with were trenches cutte : their next thwart
" neighbour, neighbour *Gravefend* was then like-
" wife fortified, and wefterne barges thither
" brought to make a bridge like to that of
" *Antwerp*, to ftop the entrance of the daring
" foe, and give free paffage both to horfe and

I   " foote

" foote betweene *Kent* and *Essex*, as occasion
" served,

" All the shires and cities of the land,
" having their trained soldiers aptly furnished
" with captaines, officers, and fit abilliments
" for warre, attended the hourely pleasure of
" the prince, *provided allways and was ever*
" *meant that all frontier ports, eyther to the*
" *sea or other station, shoulde still retaine their*
" *proper strengths, and from the inland onely to*
" *select such men, as were fittest for the generall*
" *campe.*

The land army mentioned by this author,
consisted of the following numbers, furnished
of the respective counties,

	Horsemen, Lances,	Light Horse,
Bedfordshire - -	17	40
Buckingham - -	18	83
Hartfordshire - -	25	60
Kent - - - -	50	100
Suffolk - - -	50	200
Essex - - - -	50	100

Middle-

Middlefex - - - 35   88
Surrey - - - - 8   98
         Sum 253   769

		Footmen,
Bedford	- - -	500
Buckingham	- - -	500
Hartford	- - - -	1000
Surrey	- - - - -	1000
Barkfhire	- - - - -	1000
Oxford	- - - - -	1000
London	- - - - -	1000
Suffolke	- - - - -	3000
Effex	- - - - -	5000
Kent	- - - - -	5000
Norfolke	- - - - -	3000
	Sum	22000

This number of footmen was allotted for the camp at *Tylbury*, but the number affembled amounted onely to 16500.

The armie for the guard of her Majefties perfon under the charge of the Lord Cham-

      berlayne,

berlayne, confifting both of horfe and foote, levyed out of thefe fhires following,

	Horfemen, Lances,	Light Horfe,
Gloucefter – – –	20	100
Somerfet – – –	50	100
Suffex – – – –	20	100
Wilton – – – –	25	100
Barkfhire – – –	10	85
Oxford – – – –	23	103
Cambridge – – –	13	40
Northampton – –	20	80
Leicefter – – –	9	70
Warwick – – –	17	76
Huntington – – –	6	26
Dorfet – – – –	120	0
Suffolke – – –	70	230
Norfolke – – –	80	321
Sum	481	1431

	Footemen,
Gloucefter – – –	2500
Somerfet – – – –	4000
Suffex – – – – –	2500

Wilton

Wilton – – – – –	2300
Cambridge – – – –	700
Northampton – – –	600
Leicefter – – – –	500
Warwicke – – – –	500
Huntington – – – –	400
Dorfet – – – –	1000
Suffolke – – – –	3000
Hartford – – – –	500
Surrey – – – –	500
Barkſhire – – – –	500
Oxford – – – – –	150
Worcefter – – – – –	400
Southampton – – – –	2000
Devon – – – – –	2000
London – – – –	9000
Middlefex – – – –	1000

34050

Cambden, after reciting the Naval Preparations of Queen *Elifabeth,* and proving thereby
that the wifdom of her councils had over-ruled
the infanity of thofe valourous Quixotes,
" who earneſtly perfuaded her to expect the
enemy's

enemy's coming, and to welcome him with a
land battle," proceeds to her internal arrangements, thus,

" For land fervice, there were difpofed along
" the Southern Coafts twenty thoufand men,
" befides which two armies were raifed of
" choice well difciplined men : the one under
" the command of the Earl of *Leicefter*, con-
" fifting of a thoufand horfe and twenty-two
" thoufand foot, which encamped at *Tilbury*,
" not far from the *Thames* mouth (for the
" enemy was fully refolved to fet firft upon
" *London*) the other under the leading of Lord
" *Hunfdon*, confifting of thirty-four thoufand
" foot and two thoufand horfe to guard the
" Queen's perfon.

" *Arthur* Lord *Grey*, Sir *Francis Knolles*, Sir
" *John Norris*, Sir *Richard Bingham*, and Sir
" *Roger Williams*, Knights, and excellent fol-
" diers, were made choice of, to confult about
" the beft way of managing the war at land.
" Thefe men thought good, that the moft
" convenient landing-places for the enemy, as
" well

" well out of *Spain* as out of the *Low Coun-*
" *tries*, fhould be well manned and fortified;
" namely, *Milford-Haven, Falmouth, Plymouth,*
" *Portland*, the Ifle of *Wight, Portfmouth*, that
" open coaft of *Kent* which we call the *Downs,*
" the *Thames Mouth, Harwich, Yarmouth, Hull,*
" &c. and that the trained bands all along
" the maritime counties, fhould meet in arms,
" upon a fignal given, to defend the faid parts,
" and do their beft to prohibit the enemys
" landing; and if the enemy did land, to lay
" all the country wafte round about, and to
" fpoil all things that might be of any ufe to
" them, that fo they might find no food but
" what they brought with them on their fhoul-
" ders, and to bufy the enemy night and day,
" with continual alarms, fo as to give them
" no reft, but not to put it to the hazard of
" a battle, till more commanders with their
" companies were come up to them, of which
" commanders they nominated on in every
" fhire, to have the chief command and con-
" duct. I lift not to relate, what midland
" fhires they affigned to aid this and that
" coaft

" coaſt, what numbers, what arms, and what
" manner of fight they agreed upon."

The inexhauſtible fund of ſound information, with which the annals of this period are
replete, renders it neceſſary to ſubjoin verba-
tim, the council of war as it has been tranſmitted to us, and which is preſerved in the
Britiſh Muſeum.

Council of War, held in the Year 1587.

Lord Grey,
Sir Francis Knolles, Treaſurer of the Houſe-
    hold,
Sir Thomas Laken,
Sir Walter Rawleigh,
Sir Richard Granvill,
Sir John Norris,
Sir Richard Bingham,
Sir Roger Williams,
Ralph Lane, Eſq;

Pro-

PROPOSITIONS.

Such means as are confidered to be fitteft to put the forces of the realm in order, to with-ftand an invafion; and the places moft to be fufpected, that the *Spaniards* intend to land in,

Milford,
Helford,
Falmouth,
Plymouth,
Torbay,
Portland,
The Ifle of Wight.

Thefe are apteft for the army of *Spain* to land,

Neffe, in Suffex,
The Downs,
Margate, in Kent,
The River of Thames,
Harwich,
Yarmouth,
Hull and Scotland.

K   Thefe

Thefe are apteft for the army in *Flanders*.
How many of thefe places may be put in defence, to hinder their landing.

  Milford, in Wales,
  Plymouth, for the Weft,
  Portland, for the middle of the Weft Parts;
  The Ifle of Wight,
  Portfmouth, and
  The River of Thames.

Milford,

Although we do fuppofe the barrennefs of
the country to be fuch, as it is not likely to
be invaded; yet touching *Milford-Haven*, in
refpect of the goodnefs of the fame, we think
it convenient that there fhould be trained the
number of two thoufand foot, and five hundred horfe, to be levied and had in readinefs,
and for the increafe of horfemen, if any lack
be then. The gentlemen, with their ferving-
men, may be commanded to fupply the default of the number aforefaid.

Plymouth

PLYMOUTH.

The reafon why *Plymouth* is thought to be the moft likely place, is, for that it is unlikely the King of *Spain* will engage his fleet too far within the channel, before he has maftered fome good harbour; and *Plymouth* is the neareft to *Spain*, eafy to be won, fpeedily to be by them fortified, and conveniently fituated, to fend fuccour either out of *Spain* or *France,*

PORTLAND.

The reafon why *Portland* is alfo an apt place to land in, is, for that there is a great harbour for all his fhips to ride in, and good landing for the men; the Ifle being won, is a ftrong place of retreat, and the country adjoining *Champaign*, where, with great conveniency, he may march with his whole army.

The reafon why the *Downs*, *Margate*, and the river of *Thames*, are thought fit landing-places, is, in refpect of the commodity of landing, and nearnefs to the Prince of *Parma*,

K 2   in

in whofe forces the King of *Spain* repofed fpecial truft.

Now in thefe places following, order may be taken to hinder their landing, whether by fortification, or affembly of the people, or both.

For PLYMOUTH, both by Fortification and Affembly of People.

In *Devon* and *Cornwall*, there are of trained men in the counties and ftannaries five thoufand which are to affemble for the defence of *Plymouth*, ftanding equal to both counties, of which we are of opinion, in place of mufterdays, which are very chargeable, and in effect to no purpofe, that two thoufands of thefe fhould be affembled together at *Plymouth*, under fuch a general as fhall be ordained to govern, that Weftern Army, to the intent that they may know their leaders, be acquainted, be thoroughly inftructed to all purpofes, that on fudden occafions, there may be no amaze or any confufion. This fhall be done the one half at the charge of her Majefty, the other at the

charge

charge of the country, if the country's charge do not furmount the ordinary trainings.

For PORTLAND, by affembling of Men and fortifying.

In *Dorfet* and *Wiltfhire* there are of trained men two thoufand feven hundred, which are to be affembled for the defence of that place; and that two thoufand of the faid number fhould be affembled and exercifed as before is faid, at *Plymouth*, or in fome place of *Wiltfhire*, appointed for the *Ifle of Wight*, to take *Somerfetfhire*, in which there is two thoufand foot.

At SANDWICH and THE DOWNS, by affembling of Men.

In *Kent* and *Suffex*, there are of trained men four thoufand five hundred, which are to be affembled in thofe places for defence thereof, and two thoufand of the fame number to be affembled at *Sandwich*, to be governed and exercifed as before is faid for *Plymouth*.

So likewife for *Norfolk* and *Suffolk*, like order to be obferved.

Our

Our farther meaning is, that thefe garrifons
fhall remain but twenty days to be thoroughly
trained and acquainted with encamping, and
then every fuch two thoufand men in garrifon,
being fo acquainted with difcipline, fhall give
example to a great army of raw men, whereby
fhall be no manner of confufion, on all fudden emergencies. Further, we are of opinion,
that to thefe two thoufand men, there fhall be
twenty captains appointed; which twenty captains, having each of them, one hundred trained
men, fhall receive under their charge when the
army fhall affemble, one hundred more, fo as
in effect, there fhall be four thoufand men in
order, and under martial difcipline. The choice
of which captains, we think, for the one half
to be left for the choice of the general of the
army, and the other to be of the principal gentlemen of the county, under whom there may
be foldiers appointed for their lieutenants.
The like order is to be obferved in every of
the other places of garrifon.

What Order muft be taken to fight with the
Enemy, if by force. he be landed. ·

For

For the manner how to fight with the enemy, it muſt be left to the diſcretion of the general; only we give this advice, that at his landing, he may be impeded, if conveniently it may be done; and if he march forward, that the country be driven, ſo as no victuals remain, but ſuch as they ſhall carry on their backs, which will be ſmall, that he be kept waking with continual alarms; but that in no caſe, that any battle be adventured till ſuch time as divers lieutenants be aſſembled to make a groſs army, as we have ſpecified, except upon a ſpecial advantage.

Farther, it is thought neceſſary, that in theſe two provinces, and in all others where many lieutenants be, there ſhould one be appointed to be chief, for among many lieutenants there may be ſome ſtraining of courteſy; left by ſuch delay and confuſion, great inconveniences do grow to the country, and advantages to enemy; and therefore, any lieutenant coming out of any country with his force, his authority only to extend to govern his company, as colonel of that regiment, and ſo to be commanded

manded by the general lieutenant. As for example; in *Devon* and *Cornwall*, there are ten lieutenants, whereby it may be known, who shall command in either, as need shall require.

What Proportion of Men shall be prepared to serve that End.

Wheresoever the enemy shall land, as if at *Plymouth* for example, then by the computation of six thousand men, armed and furnished in *Devon* and *Cornwall*, we conceive that the assistance of *Wiltshire*, *Dorset*, and *Somerset*, adjoing to the six thousand of the *West*, will make a sufficient army, being strengthened by the gentlemen, and serving-men, and other of the country that shall be adjoined, though not so thoroughly armed as the *West*; and if it happen, either by design or contrary weather, that the enemy pass over *Plymouth*, and land at *Portland*, then the armed men and trained soldiers of the *West*, shall repair to them; and further, if the invasion be in *Kent*, or any other ways to the West of the River of *Thames*, then

then thofe middle fhires directed to affift the *Weft*, may turn to the *Eaft*, along the coaft.

If the army of *Flanders* land in the River of *Thames*, then the fame order is to be taken with the fhires adjoining as is aforefaid; namely, *Suffolk*, *Norfolk*, *Effex*, and the City of *London*. And becaufe there is a fpecial regard to be had of her Majefty's perfon, we think it moft neceffary that an army fhould be provided to that end, to be compofed of fuch counties as are appointed and referved for that purpofe, and to join with the forces of the City of *London* and fuch others, as may be armed out of her Majefty's ftores.

Farthermore, for the increafe of foot, lacking armour, we think it fit that there be of able men unarmed, whereof choice may be made of the trained men armed, one fourth part more of which fourth part of unarmed men, eighty may be pikes, and twenty billmen, for the providing of which pikes and bills, there muft be fpeedy provifion made, being weapons that the realm doth furnifh.

L   Alfo

Alfo for the increafe of armed pikemen, in this time of fcarcity of armour, we do think it good, that all the armed bill-men may be converted to be made armed pikemen, and that all able bill-men unarmed, fhould be levied and chofen in their places, becaufe the ranks of bill-men in order of battle, are always environed and encompaffed about with pikemen, for the bill-men ferve efpecially for execution, if the enemy in battle fhall be overthrown. But, here it is to be noted, that there muft be referved a few armed bill-men and halberdiers, to guard the ranks, wherein the enfigns, drums, &c. are placed in order of battle.

Alfo, fince upon any fudden invafion, it would be too late to provide thefe things which fhall be neceffary for defence, it is thought neceffary that before-hand, a ftore of ordnance and ammunition be provided, as alfo powder-fpades, and all other furniture whatfoever; and to be left in thefe fore-named places, in which there garrifons fhall remain; it is alfo to be provided, that in all thofe general affemblies be held for training as well horfemen as
footmen;

footmen; and to that end, that at *Plymouth*, *Portland*, *Sandwich*, and any other places, that shall be fit to have the like training, the horse-men of the next adjoining counties be brought together: as namely, at *Plymouth*, those of *Devon*, *Cornwall*, and *Somerset*; at *Portland*, those of *Dorset*, and *Wiltshire*, *Hampshire*, and *Berkshire*; at *Sandwich*, those of *Kent*, *Suffex*, *Surry*, *&c.* But because it may fall out in those places appointed for training of the infantry, they may want forage, or place fit for horsemen, it may be left to the discretion of the lieutenants, tho chuse the fittest for the cavalry, as near the foot as conveniently they may.

Scotland.

Farther, as touching *Scotland*, where landing we cannot resist, we think it meet that a stronger proportion be considered of, for that part; namely six thousand foot, and two thousand horse, whereof to be a thousand lances; arms of far more defence, and may be furnished as good and cheap as the jack, and to be taken out of the tower.

L 2

' If therefore, the army of *Flanders* fhould happen to land in *Scotland,* whereby their force and ftrength fhall be fo great, as the army aforefaid fhall not be able to encounter them; then we think fit that a good part of the army prepared to guard her Majefty's perfon, fhall march to fupport the army of the *North,* againft that enemy; and joined with the trained of that country, and the army of the *Weft* brought to fupply that charge.

It is alfo moft carefully to be confidered, that the King of *Spain,* is not hopelefs of fome party of *Papifts* and malecontents.

All which, if thefe fmall regiments before fpoken of, be not in readinefs, both to affemble for refiftance of any foreign enemy, and to withftand them at home both in one day; for every man fhall ftand in fear of firing of his own houfe, and deftruction of his family: Therefore, if any ftir fhould happen, fuch fevere proceedings or execution towards fuch offenders, would be ufed by martial law.

And

And to conclude, when it fhall be bruited in *Spain*, that there are at *Plymouth*, and other places, fuch a number of armed foldiers, under enfigns and leaders, the number will be reported to be double or treble; fo as the King of *Spain*, upon good probability, may concieve, that thefe foldiers, and fuch as are in other places upon the coaft, in like readinefs are determined to land in *Portugal* or the *Indies*; the fame opinion being fortified by the preparation of fo many fhips as are given in charge to be made ready in thofe parts, by Sir *Francis Drake*.

We think it alfo very neceffary, that throughout all the countries of the realm, this proportion as well amongft the armed and trained as the unarmed, pikes and bills may be obferved; that is to fay, that of every hundred there be eighty. pikes, and twenty bills.

We think it neceffary that fome order and provifion be alfo taken by their lordfhips, that

her

her Majesty's ships being at *Rochester* be not
entrapped."

Then follows an arrangement of bill-men
and pike-men, with their difposition in companies of one hundred each and the appointment of a chief, under such title, as shall
seem good to the Lords of the Council, to be
affifted with a fufficient number of experienced
captains to be in her Majesty's pay. The said
chief gentleman to give fuch orders for the
training and exercifing the faid regiment, with
the affiftance of the said experienced captains,
as shall seem good unto him, and also for
training the horfemen.

This ends the Council of War.———Dated.
27th Nov. 1587.

From *Stowe's* account, it appears, that the
forces in readinefs, amounted to 58,984 men.
And he adds, " yet there were ready in all
places, many thoufands more to back and fecond them.

Cambden,

Cambden alfo in round numbers tells us, there were 59,000 in the two armies, befides 20,000 difpofed along the *Southern* coafts. Lord *Bacon* too fays, that befides the levies actually embodied, " There were alfo other dormant " mufters of foldiers throughout all parts of " realm that were put in readinefs, but not " drawn together."

To what immenfe numbers thefe might amount, may be gathered from a manufcript in the *Cottonian* collection, which relates the number of able men returned to government to be in the *English* counties, 298,068. In the *Welch*, 18,026; and in the cities and towns corporate, 5472.——I have alfo fubjoined to the appendix, an incompleat abftract of the lord lieutenants certificates of them and their array; befides all which, the levies of individuals were prodigious.

I have taken the pains to decypher a variety of papers, fome extracts of which cannot be uninterrefting; either as eftablifhing the fyftem of defence, or fhewing the wifdom of the fovereign,

vereign, asking and courteously receiving, the opinions of all; and the universal ardour which pervaded the whole nation.

Lord-keeper Sir *Nicholas Bacon* to Queen *Elizabeth*, 20th. *Nov*. 1557. " ——and con- " cerning matters at home, I think that your " Highness's musters be continued, and their " certificates carefully perused; and thereupon " order taken from time to time, to supply " all wants, as well of captains, munition, " men, and armour, against all sudden chances.

" I trust there shall be small cause of fear, " for any want at home."

Lord North to the Lord-treasurer.—1587.

" Now, my good lord, knowing no man " living, more careful for the service of her " Majesty than yourself, I come only to you, " letting your lordship know, that this county " of *Cambridge*, and the Isle of *Ely*, which " reacheth to the sea, is put in no readiness, " either of men, horses, or armour; there " hath been no muster or view taken here " these three or four years. All other shires

" about

" about us, mufter, arm, and put in readinefs,
" what they can poffibly. To have the forces
" of this place in like readinefs, if your lord-
" fhip thinks fo good were convenient, the
" fooner the better, that men may have time
" to furnifh themfelves, not law-like, but lov-
" ingly to furnifh themfelves after a reafona-
" able rate, which no doubt will be done here
" very dutifully. Your good Lordfhip will
" pardon me if I exceed my bounds; love
" to her Majefty's Service moveth me to put
" your Lordfhip in mind thereof."

The pains taken to roufe the people, and
apprize them of their danger, were not merely
confined to the pulpit, for a letter from the
Queen herfelf to the Lord Lieutenant of *Lan-
cafhire* bids him enforce; " how every man's
" particular eftate is threatened in the higheft
" degree to be touched in refpect of country,
" liberty, wyffe, children, lands, lyffe and re-
" ligion; and looking that moft of them fhould
" have upon this inftant extraordinary occafion
" a larger proportion of furniture for foot and
" horfe than hath been certified."——

A

A letter from the lords of the council to the Earl of *Bath*, Lord Lieutenant of the county of *Devon* :——" directs him to fortify the ifland of *St. Nicholas*, and fays that in regard of the late warnings, it cannot be but that they are very alert and prepared, and therefore when it is once put in a pofture of defence, he may for the eafe of the country let them go home, ordering thefe of the neareft villages to be conftantly in readinefs to throw themfelves into it upon an hours warning, confidering alfo what numbers fhould conftantly remain to prevent a fudden furprize,—and he is further ordered to fend boats to lie along to the weftward to make fignals to the coaft.————

As a proof how early the plans of defence were adopted, the following are minutes of orders fent to the Lord Lieutenant in 1585.

To caufe a view to be taken of all places of defence, and to confider what fconces, or other kind of defence may be made there, without any great charge to the county; and that the enemy may be impeached in landing.

To

To confider if the landing places fhould be taken, what ftreights and other apt places, there are to make head againft him.

To appoint by way of diftribution, certain of the trained men and others, to repair to the faid places. To make choice of certain pioneers to refort unto the places of defence. To fee the beacons erected, and well kept. To fend certificates of the ftate of the county.

Further minutes of council about the fame time, are, *That except it be a general mufter of the whole county, no man may be compelled to go above feven or eight mliesto train, in his own divifion.* That upon any invafion, the foldiers may repair to the next captain's dwelling upon the fea coafts, and not go to their own captain, who dwelleth fome ten miles within land, and leave the coaft unfurnifhed.

That order be taken, that arms may be ferved at reafonable rates at the armourer's office at *Plymouth.*

That

That an act or order be taken, that all muskets and piftols be of a bore, and that thofe hereafter charged may find fuch; that the match, powder, and bullets, may be kept in fome fit place in each divifion, to be ready when need fhall require, and to be had at the King's price, as formerly.

There are alfo, orders to confult with experienced perfons of the country, and confultations with the Lord-lieutenants, about quartering the troops, defiring their opinions, which this council was not afhamed of afking. Taxes were levied in the different hundreds, for watching their beacons, and inftructions fent to the Lord Mayor to prefs Weft-country barges, to fortify the *Thames*; and the fame care was extended to all the Southern ports: for there are accounts of no lefs than seventeen forts and caftles, fpecified in the county of *Suffex* alone.

Some other interefting papers are referred to the Appendix, together with the inftructions iffued to the Lord-lieutenants of counties,

which

which display such admirable wisdom of good policy, as leaves me to regret that part is yet wanting, which all my endeavours to discover, have been ineffectual.

Having seen what were the armaments of this kingdom, let us turn to those of the enemy, according to the best accounts handed down, which is related as follows.

I omit what belongs to the naval department, having only to mention the troops which could be opposed to those of the country.

Camden relates the number of soldiers on board the *Armada*   -   -   19,290
  Strype ditto   -   -   -   19,295
  Stowe ditto   -   -   -   20,000

Besides these, the Duke of *Parma* had with him 30,000, and the Duke of *Guise* was to have brought 12,000 more, but these were very early disbanded. And it is more than probable these numbers would have fallen very short in effective fighting men, if we are to judge

from

from the following ftate of the lumber which
encumbered the grand part of the expedition

Relation of the fhippes, munition, victuals and
men both foldiers and mariners, of the army
of *Spaine*. Printed in *Lifburne* and prefented
to the King, the 9th day of *May*, 1558.

Soldiers — — — —	18973
Mariners — — — —	8050
Volunteer Gentlemen — .—	124
Their Servants — — —	464
Gentlemen ferving for Pay —	238
Their Servants — — —	163
Gunners and their Mates — —	167
Surgeons and Barbers: — —	85
Friars and Orders to Prayer —	180
Gentlemen of the Duke's Houfe	22
Their Servants — — —	50
Mufterers and Overfeers — —	17
Their Servants — — —	50
Juftices to execute Juftice — —	19
In the Gallies and Galliaffes to row with Oars — — —	2088
Total	**30,655**

Ab-

Abſtract of a Paper tranſmitted to the Lords Lieutenant.

From the *Sloan.* Manuſcripts.

A Note what forces ſhall repair to the principal havens in every county upon the ſea-
coaſt, when the enemy ſhall attempt to take
land; which forces are to be taken of the
beſt and beſt furniſhed men in every ſhire.

Men appointed to repair to *Falmouth* in
Cornwall, when any enemy ſhould attempt
to land. Their men to be employed there,
or in other places of the ſhore where moſt
need ſhall be.

FALMOUTH,	From Cornwall	4000
	Devon -	4000
	Somerſet	3000
	Total	11000

Men appointed to repair to *Plymouth* in
Devonſhire, when any enemy ſhould attempt
to land, there to be employed.

PLY-

PLYMOUTH,	Devon	-	6000
	Cornwall	-	2000
	Dorfet	-	3000
	Somerfet	-	4000
	Wilts	- -	2000
			17000
POOLE,	Dorfet	- -	4000
	Devon	-	4000
	Somerfet	-	4000
	Wilts	- -	2000
			14000
PORTSMOUTH,	Hants	- -	4000
	Wilts	- -	2000
	Berks	- -	3000
	Suffex	- -	4000
	Surrey	-	3000
			16000
Any Port in SUSSEX,	Suffex	-	7000
	Hants	- -	3000
	Kent	, -	4000
	Surrey	-	3000
			15000

Ifle

Isle of SHEPPEY,	Kent	- -	6000
or KENT,	Suffex	-	4000
	Surrey	-	3000
	London	-	3000
	Effex	- -	4000
			20000

HARWICH,	Effex	- -	6000
	Kent	- -	4000
	London	-	3000
	Hertford	-	1000
	Cambridge and Ely		700
	Suffolk	-	3000
			17700

YARMOUTH,	Norfolk	-	6000
	Suffolk	-	4000
	Lincoln	-	3000
	Cambridge	-	700
	Huntingdon	-	300
			14000

N   SUF-

SUFFOLK,	Suffolk	-	7000
	Norfolk	-	3000
	Effex	- -	4000
	Cambridge	-	500
-	Huntingdon	-	300
	Herts	- -	500
			15300

It was the good policy of this reign, to make ufe of talents wherever they could be found; and accordingly, the moft intelligent gentlemen of each county were applied to for information, relative to the principal circumftances in their vicinity. And I had an opportunity of admiring the importance of fuch a meafure, in the extreme attention paid by two country gentlemen, to a large extent of coaft; the furvey of which is preferved in a private library, and contains the moft exact delineation and account of the fhoals, rocks, clifts, beacons, and landing places, with remarks upon works made or intended, the return of cannon and ammunition, and many obfervations on the ftrength or weak-

weaknefs of pofts, which even at this day, it would not be prudent to publifh.———Befides this, men of approved abilities, were fent down by the council, whofe bufinefs cannot be better explained, than by fubjoining their inftructions as follows.

HARLEAN MS. 4228 p. 38 b.
Inftructions given to Sir *John Norris*, and other martial men, fent into the maritime countrie, the 12th of *April*, 1588.

For as much as it is greatly to be doubted, that in cafe the enemy fhould make any attempt or difcent, into any of the maritime counties, for lack of fome good eftablifhed order, both for the impeachment of his landing and difcent, and the choife of fome apt and fit places for retreat of forces to withftand him, and for erecting the body of an army to make head againft him, great confufion is like to fall out, to the difmaying of the good fubjects, and the encouraging of the enemy. It is thought meet by her Majefty, that fome perfons of fkill and judgment, fhould be fent down to confer

with

with the feveral lieutenants of the maritime counties, for the eftablifhing of fome fuch good orders; whereby the confufion likely to enfue, may be avoided. And for that there hath been fpecial choife made of you, in refpect of your fkill in martial affairs, to take a view of the counties of A, B, C, D. you fhall with as much fpeed as you may, make your repair to the faid counties, beginning at the county of A, and fo to continue and proceed in the viewing of the faid feveral counties, until you fhall have finifhed the fervice according to the directions hereafter following.

Firft, you fhall receive our letters, directed to the feveral fheriffs of the counties committed to your charge, by the which they are required to notify unto the lieutenant of the feveral counties, that her Majefties pleafure is, that they repair to their towns of each county, or to the principal place in the faid county, ufually accuftomed for fuch affembly, to meet with you at fuch time, as by your particular letter fhall be fignified unto the faid fheriff; you fhall at the affembly make the faid lieutenants,

nants, or their deputies, acquainted with the caufe of your repair thither, and require them by virtue of fuch letters as you fhall receive from her Majeftie for that purpofe, to affift you in the fervice committed to your charge.

And firft, for the viewing of the places of defcent, you fhall let them underftand that her Majefties pleafure is, that both they and you fhail repair to the faid places, accompanied only with fuch perfons as have fkill, and men of truft, for it is thought convenient, that there fhould not be many acquainted with the danger and weaknefs of the faid places.

And after a view taken of the faid places, you fhall, after conference had with the faid lieutenants, deliver unto the faid lieutenants, in writing, your beft advice for the impeaching of the enemies defcent; as alfo how the forces of the country may make their retreat with fafety and honour, to fuch places of ftrength, as by you fhall be thought meet.

Amongft

Amongst other things, it shall be very re-
quisite, that some of the best trayned bands
within that county, and best furnished with
martial men, be appointed to impeach the
said descent, to be executed according to such
directions as by you shall be given to the said
lieutenants, with the advice of such captains
as you shall leave there to assist the lieutenants,
and to see due execution of such advice as you
shall leave with them in writing.

After the view of the said places of descent,
you shall then consider of some fit place within
the said counties, that by the situation, with the
help of some rivers or other straights, shall be
most fit, with the use and assistance of the pioneers, to be put in some such strength, as may
be able to make head unto the enemy, and to
stay his incursions until such time as the forces
of other counties appointed to yield assistance,
shall repair thither; as also, until they shall
receive orders and directions from her Majestie,
how to proceed, and deal with the enemy.

And

And forasmuch as nothing will be more neceffary for the ftrengthening fuch places of defence upon the fuddain, than the ufe of many
pioneers, and other artificers, you fhall require
the faid lieutenants in her Majefties name, to
take a fpecial care, to have fuch numbers of
pioneers in a readinefs, as by you fhall be
thought fufficient for the ftrengthening the faid
places of retreat; and to fee that there be provifion made of mattocks, fpades, fhovels, and
all other neceffaries fit to be ufed and employed
in that fervice, by the fame pioneers: you
fhall alfo give directions unto the fame lieutenants, how fuch horfemen as are within the
fame counties, may be beft employed in the
champion or plaine places of the faid counties, as well for the annoying of the enemy,
as for the defence in the retreat of fuch bands,
as fhall be ufed in the impeaching of the enemies defcent: you fhall alfo take a view in the
faid counties, of the feveral bands, both horfemen and footmen; and in cafe you fhall find
them not fufficiently trayned, or not that choce
made of the men, or not fo fufficiently furnifhed with armour and weapon, as apper-

taineth

taineth, you fhall require the faid lieutenants, in her Majefties name, to fee the faid defects reformed, and to take order with the faid captains whom you fhall leave in the faid counties, as well to put the faid lieutenant to fee fpeedy redrefs of the faid defects; as alfo to employ themfelves in the trayning of the faid bands, as well horfe as foot.

Amongft other matters of importance to be obferved, you fhall confer with the faid lieutenants, in cafe the enemy fhould take footing, on land, how there may be good order taken, for the removing into the inland parts of the country, of all manner of cattle, victuals, and other neceffaries, that may in any fort relieve the enemy; and to fee the places of retreat furnifhed with a convenient portion of victuals for the number of forces that fhall be there placed.

For execution whereof, it fhall be meet that fome fpecial perfons fhall be appointed, that fhall be men of credit and difcretion, fit for that fervice, for that otherwife, it is likely there
will

will fall out a great confufion; you fhall alfo confer with the faid lieutenants, about the due execution of fome neceffary points contained in former inftructions, as have been heretofore given unto them, whereof you fhall have a copy, fo far forth as they fhall not be found repugnant to thefe prefents.

And for her Majefties fatisfaction in the mean time, untill you return, you fhall certify from time to time, how you find the ftate of the feveral counties, after you have taken a view of them, and fhall fend a copy of fuch directions as you fhall leave with the faid lieutenants.

And whereas this fervice might feem to require many other particular directions; forasmuch as by thefe inftructions, it might appear unto you, that her Majefties intention is to have the forces of thefe counties to be made apt, and in readinefs for a fervice, and all things neceffary for defence provided accordingly; upon conference with the lieutenants or deputies, and view of the forces, and ftate of

O

the

the countries, you fhall be able to confider and conceive, what you think further meet to be done in that behalf. Wherein, and in all things meet to adorn this fervice, you fhall give your beft advice to the faid lieutenants and direction for executing that which fhall be thought requi-fite.

Convinced, that nothing I can offer, would be fo interefting as this hiftoric authentication of the principles of defenfive war in general, and their immediate application to this parti-cular ifland. I fhall be juftified in fhewing the teftimony of another hiftorian, whofe expref-fions are ftrong enough to carry a conviction, how the conduct of this great princefs, has ever impreffed the minds of thofe who thought upon the fubject.

Rapin fays, that befides the armies there was in each county a body of militia well armed, under leaders who had orders to join one ano-ther as occafion fhould require. The fea ports were fortified, as much as the time would per-mit, and fignals were every where appointed to fhow the places where the troops were to march.—In fhort, it was refolved that if the *Spaniards* made a defcent, the country about them fhould be laid wafte, that they might have nothing to fubfift upon but what they brought from the fleet. This was the 'courfe taken by *Francis* I. in *Provence* againft *Charles* V. with a fuccefs that anfwered his expecta-tion. Thefe meafures being taken the enemy was expected with uncommon alacrity, though it fhould feem that on fuch an occafion every one fhould have been in the utmoft confter-nation.

The hiftorian afterwards expreffes the Queen's juft dread, becaufe if fhe could not hinder the *Spaniards* from landing in *England*, fhe muft neceffarily refolve to hazard a battle, the country not being proper to prolong the war.—But he allows if ever fhe difcovered abi-lity, it was on this important occafion, for fhe looked to every thing with a wonderful prudence and a prefence of mind, rarely to be found in the greateft men, and which gained her the admiration and praifes of all the world.

From

From this view of the tranfaction of the year 1588, it will clearly be deduced that Queen *Elizabeth* and her minifters adjudged a general line of defence neceffary to be traced out and adopted beforehand, and that they according-ly did adopt fuch a plan: that their mea-fures were wife, and falutary; formed on true principles, and ought to be adverted to in fimilar fituations.—That intelligent perfons were every where confulted; and the inhabi-tants countenanced to affociate a confiderable time *(Stowe* fays three years) beforehand. That the fyftem of harraffing the enemy, deftroying forage, throwing up entrenchments, and avoid-ing battle was particularly inculcated. *That the troops of the maritime counties were ftudioufly appoint d to the defence of their own coafts,* and that the Queen took all thefe precautions not-withftanding fhe had an active navy, which alone under God defeated the armada, and a land force *actually embodied* fuperior to what was bringing againft her.——Thefe are part of the material deductions this narrative affords; the intelligent reader will find fo many others, that he will pardon the pointing thefe out, in

con-

confideration of the numbers who in reading hiftory retain faithfully all its *events,* without extracting one folid opinion, or maturing their judgment by a fingle reflection, which is but the triumph of memory over the underftand-ing.——How much better would it be if our youth were inftructed to confider facts as but the fcaffold to a nobler ftructure. The inflexi-bility of an impartial magiftrate, the *Juftice to herfelf fevere* might be derived from a former impreffion without immediately recollecting *Brutus,* and even if the name of *Lycurgus* were forgotten, a conviction might remain that the love of pleafure, and the dread of fhame were powerful fprings of action, one of which is wholly unknown to modern legiflators, the other rarely applied to.——If the records of antiquity are merely to be turned over for the adventures they contain, they fhould be ap-propriated to the ufe of nurferies, fome old goffip made *Cuftos Rotulorum,* and *Tom Thumb* would be the firft of hiftories.—The human mind being only capable of retaining and com-bining a finite quantity of intellectual matter there needs little hefitation to pronounce, that

it

it should consist of the most valuable and refined substance ; hence chronology is the very
chaff of literature.—The defects of our public
education in this point, are perhaps without
remedy; but that those entrusted with the
charge of a single pupil should stuff his head
with the rubbish of words, dates, and names,
is not to be forgiven.—Necessity has furnished
a wiser system for arts and manufactures, a
painter, a musician apply at once to the instru-
ments of their profession. A carpenter uses
those tools by which he is to earn his bread,
but the art of employing reason, which is to be
the end of scientific education, forms no part
of it. *Rousseau* indeed taught his *Emile* to
think for himself, but he thinks for himself
only; without extending his ideas sufficiently
to the relative establishments of society. This
principle of diving constantly beyond the sur-
face for somewhat to bear off, explodes all
trifling.—The mind habituated to substance
grasps at no shadows. This at once let *De Retz*
into the character that could observe how many
years the same pen had been employed.—This
taught *Alexander* to reward with a bushel of
corn,

corn, the man whofe merit confifted in toffing the grains through the eye of a bodkin. To appreciate the fterling value of things is furely the grand object; and for want of this knowledge there exifts at this day a man of great reading, who can tell the author, date, printer, price, edition, and fize of almoft every book extant, without having ever made the fmalleft enquiry into the contents of any of them.— What fuch intenfe application might have atchieved, is lefs material than to obferve, that he, who abforbed in folid reflection fhould even confound *William the Conqueror* with *William Prince of Orange*, would in point of fcience fcarce appear lefs refpectably verfed in hiftory, than the more fafhionable reader whofe head unembarraffed by meditation retained every date, without one remark on the origin of power, and thofe breaches of the focial contract, under which it was delegated that fanctified the Revolution; or who views the *Norman* conqueft without perceiving its effects on our laws and cuftoms, or obferving that *Harold* facrificed his crown and his life to an ignorance of the firft principles of denfenfive war.

CHAP.

C H A P. IV.

*General Idea of Defence.—Utility
of Affociation.*

TO fuppofe a plan of operations for an enemy who fhould land in this country, would be abfurd in him who wanted abilities, and attended with worfe confequences from the foldier who poffeffed them. But a few general remarks either on matters notorioufly public or palpably obvious, may awaken attention at home, without conveying other information abroad than it would be ridiculous to conceive an enemy unpoffeffed of. It may therefore be faid, that as the fouth and weftern coafts offer the neareft and moft advantageous footing to the Houfe of *Bourbon*, its attacks would probably be directed to fome of thofe;

whilft

whilſt, if a ſpirit of enterprize ſeize the *Dutch* the eaſtern part of the iſland preſents a ſhore well known, and invitingly contiguous.—It is unfortunately needleſs to debate whether the *Engliſh* navy be in a ſituation to block up an armament, which is within the recollection of better days ; but were thoſe days to return, *Holland* might have a ſhare in the buſineſs not ſo pleaſant to deal with ; there is no riding near her ſhores in bad weather, and the ſame winds that could waft them hither would effectually oppoſe our fleets meeting them.— Again while *Spithead* is our head quarters, if our weſterly trade winds ſet in, what ſecures the weſtern counties from *Breſt* or *L'Orient.*

The want of a ſufficient object is indeed a conſideration at ſuch a diſtance from the capital, eſpecially as *Plymouth* warned by her miraculous eſcape, is too ſtrong for a *coup de main,* and we have too much cavalry for an enemy to think of penetrating through *Dorſetſhire* or *Hants.*—*Suſſex* and *Kent* are full of poſts, that might be defended by the inhabitants, provided their own militia were left to

P   ſecond

ſecond them, and the principal force of the realm has been very properly diſtributed Eaſt of the capital.—Notwithſtanding my profeſſing to diſcuſs nothing but topics univerſally known, I have been prevailed on to mutilate this chapter, by obliterating all obſervations on ſpecific enterpriſes, or particular diſtricts. I ſhall therefore proceed to obſerve that, beſides the great general principles of defenſive war, there are certain conſiderations of no leſs moment, adapted to the peculiar ſituation, ſoil, extent, and government of every country. Of theſe, examples but too recent may be derived from *America* and the *Weſt Indies*. In the firſt, a prodigious tract of dominion, thinly peopled, and partially cultivated, throws a very ſmall portion of national wealth into the hands of an enemy. An inroad of an hundred miles produces comparatively the moſt trifling devaſtations. While in the iſlands all this is preciſely reverſed, the growing crop, the utenſils, the negroes, and the buildings bear ſuch a vaſt proportion to the value of the territory itſelf, that all ſyſtem of defenſive war becomes totally impracticable. The chance of an immediate

diate engagement is the only refource of the
inhabitants, and its event at once decides all
conteft.—Between thefe, *Great Britain* fteers a
kind of middle courfe, equally incapable of
fupporting all the confequences of continental
conduct ; and preferved from the defperate ex-
pofure of *Weft Indian* neceffity.—It is therefore obvious, that her defenfive operations muft
partake of both, And if the inroads of an invader are to be limitted without the dangerous
experiment of a battle, it muft be atchieved
by fuch univerfal preparations of refiftance, as
may impede his progrefs, and raife a feries of
obftacles conftantly accumulating, till they become infurmountable.—Thefe are not the production of an hour. Nothing but a garrifoned
fortrefs or a compleat overthrow, occafions an
immediate check. The firft we are not furnifhed with. The latter muft not be hazarded
while the controul of fortune may decide the
victory which fkill and valour have in vain
contefted. Whoever has ftudied the geography
of this ifland with a military eye, will forefee
an event far within the fcale of human poffibility ; it is, that an enemy wholly up-impeded

by

by the efforts of the neighbourhood, may in certain fituations be able to penetrate fo far, before our army could take poft in force, as to render it impoffible for that army to cover the capital without an engagement.—A particular fpot unfortified can only be maintained by an action, at the will of thofe who mean to carry it. All operations of delay allow fome lofs of ground, and the lofing ground neceffarily fuppofes a fcope, and choice of interior pofts, which every mile does not furnifh.——There are cafes when the retarding an enemy's progrefs for a fingle day, might affemble and afford the *Britifh* army every fituation it wifhed for. It is therefore of momentous importance, that the obftructions be immediate. Not to oppofe the very landing would be madnefs, and with reluctance the melancholy fact is extorted, that at this inftant they are places wherein it might be effected by almoft any number, without a fingle fhot being fired, after three years alarm of projected invafions.

Admitting therefore, as we muft, the poffibility of this being atchieved; it would be

unwife

unwife to reject the fmalleft affiftance, or to
conclude that becaufe a body of armed peafants
were not likely to repell the enemy, they could
not annoy him ; when the very fhadow of refiftance would have weight, and would compel
fuch manœvures and arrangements as muft
breed inconceivable delay. A ploughman may
at leaft break down a bridge as effectually as
Vauban himfelf could have done it ; and his
neighbours may be equally active in deftroying
the roads that would conduct pontoons to the
river ; perhaps too a few volunteers firing from
the oppofite bank might oblige him to bring
up cannon before they were diflodged,

Hence the propriety of armed affociations,
a meafure which we have feen *Queen Elizabeth*
wifely promoting : and if we confider the
names that compofed her council, and the
fuccefsful refult of their proceedings, perhaps
even our more enlightened miniftry need not
hold them abfolutely in contempt.

To carry the plan of affociation generally
into execution, little, more is neceffary than
for

for government to trace out one regular rational outline; which it would be hard not to give them credit for, confidering the variety of modes in which it might be defigned, and the numerous expedients for giving it the neceffary ftability,—Let us fuppofe a legiflature entering philofophically into the fources of human conduct, and difcovering, that a manly candid ftate of our internal refources would appeal to the underftanding of the wife; that a new and interefting employ would awaken the curiofity of the light; that opportunities of public exhibition would allure the vain; and fome well devifed honorary diftinctions, however trifling, feathers, medals, or cockades of different gradations of colour would operate upon all. The human heart is in no ftate infenfible to glory, To command the attention of an applauding fenate, to roar the beft catch in a drunken club, have each their charms; and the moft dexterous in a gang of pickpockets has as much envy in his way, as ever the juftice of *Ariftides* excited, and probably more rivals.

Let

Let not therefore the pride of pompous affectation raife a contemptuous fneer, at the homely rewards of village virtue. To have their actions recited in the fongs of dancing virgins, foftered all the *Spartan* heroifm. Perhaps the name of the moft meritorious affociator recorded in gilt letters, in a country church, would tranfmit a local reputation to his pofterity, as much emulated as any honours hiftory can beftow on thofe who move in higher orbits. *England,* thus arrayed, could never afford an opportunity of difplaying perfonal intrepidity in real action, to decide thefe claims, for no power on earth, would venture to invade her; therefore, a conftant attendance at the exercifes, and expertnefs in them, might be the merits to deferve diftinction, and the mode of conferring it fairly, might be borrowed from the Oftracifm of the *Athenians.*

Without entering into a minute detail of any one plan, it is evident, on thefe principles, many might be adopted, to furnifh *Great Britain* with an army, confifting of every inhabitant capable of the operations of defenfive war;

war; which includes infinitely more than thofe
fit to bear arms, for the aged and children·
in retiring, might drive off the cattle, and the
women themfelves could make cartridges, light
beacons, &c. if fuch exertions could by any poffibility be required. However, without ferioufly
propofing to employ females in this line, it
,is to be wifhed the policy of this country had
been fuch, as to have reftored by their means,
an immenfe number of men to the fervice of the
community, who are ignobly ftolen from it by
feminine profeffions. An effective man making
ftays, perriwigs, or gloves, is throwing away
Hercules at a diftaff; at any period it is ridiculous, in thefe days it fhould be criminal. In
every commercial ftate, the aggregate of private coutributions to the public wealth, fhould
be a *maximum*; at leaft, it will be the nearer
perfection, as the refult of individuals labour
approaches to the greateft poffible. But if we
employ a crane to raife a pincufhion, our me·
chanic powers are ill employed. I fhall hardly
take upon me to fay, what women are not fit
for, having feen them at *Teignmouth*, become
excellent mariners; and in other countries per-
forming

forming all the operations of hufbandry, while
in this, it is furely hard upon the fex, to be almoft entirely reftrained to the profeffions of
milliners, mantua-makers, or proftitutes, and
even to have thefe encroached upon.

The neceffities of the ftate, in every age,
have awakened the feelings of its members.
Danger can give activity to the fupine, and vi-
gour to the weak. Fertile in expedients, and
rapid in its execution, its approach calls forth
new refources.—No fooner had the hoftile ban-
ners of *Bourbon* appeared off *Plymouth*, than the
whole weftern coaft was in the field, and as if
fome new *Cadmus* had fown his ferpents teeth,
the country teemed with armed men. Not a
village but prefented its volunteer company,
not a hamlet but affociated with the next. Fifteen hundred men raifed in a few hours, by one
gentlemen * and his neighbours, fet off inftant-
ly with a numerous body of prifoners, and after
the fatigues of three days very unpleafant march,
were not diffatisfied at being obliged to guard

* Mr. Baftard, of Kitely.

Q   them

them all night in the fields. When they arrived at *Exeter*, the inhabitants of that city,
had already formed themfelves into five fuch
companies, for character, refpectability of fortune, as perhaps, were never before affembled.
Thefe with moft diftinguifhed humanity, were
drawn up in readinefs, to relieve their exhaufted
neighbours, the moment they arrived; and continued guarding the prifoners feveral weeks,
with unremitted attention; gentlemen of the
beft property, taking their tour to ftand centi-
nel as regularly, and difcharging the duty at
leaft as faithfully, as any high-dreffed foldier
whatever.

This was beginning to make the efforts of
the country appear refpectable; had the enemy
remained, a very fhort time would have rendered them formidable; and doubly fo they
might have been, if any fyftem had been
adopted beforehand, or any arrangements made
to unite the gallantry of individuals, and direct
its efforts to the general good. For want of
this, thoufands remained inactive, with both
the wifhes and abilities for fervice.—Others
again

again felt the neceffity of concentrating their force, and affembling in bodies; ftill without an object, but burning with fuch an ardour to be ufeful, that folly herfelf would call it mad-nefs, to difqualify them for it in future.

In every ftate liable to invafion, armed affo-ciations fhould be early adopted and encou-raged, on every principle of patriotic prudence. The word Patriotic, is ufed with no party de-fignation. To minifters themfelves, I cannot hefitate to attribute that patriotifm, which would protect this country from tyranny, or any op-preffions but their own, and even faction would unite in any well-formed plan, for national fe-curity. Yet it has been held out as the lan-guage of the day, that the people are not to be trufted with arms. A doctrine illegal, im-politic, and which can only originate in guilt or error. The univerfal underftanding of an enlightened nation, is furely to be depended on. Corruption or depravity may influence the con-duct of the ruling few, and direct the force of the unhappy nation they mifguide, againft its own colonies; but when the many are left to

Q 2   the

the operation of their reafon, their weapons
can only threaten the enemies of their country,
And fhould a race nurtured in its bofom, merit
that ungracious appellation? Heaven forbid,
their being minifters would fcreen them from
the vengeance of an injured people! However
cherifhed, however protected, the very hand
that raifed them is impotent to break their fall.
Much indeed, has been faid and written, on the
enervated depravity of the age; but diffipation,
however hoftile to the redundance of that virtue which diftinguifhed our illuftrious anceftors, ftill leaves a fpring to actuate the minds
of their defcendents, however unconfcious of
its power, however weakened in it. There are
refources, which a torpid infenfibility alone can
deftroy; and that ftate can never be the lot of
England, fo long as the very form of her conftitution is preferved. The liberty of the prefs
alone, becomes the *Palladium* of our feelings,
and guarantees us from the danger of inertnefs.
The fanguine animation of individuals may anticipate the hour of danger, but the folid fpirit of the nation kindles at the inftant of its
arrival. A certain latent fpark pervades every
                                        rank,

rank, and infpires every breaft; fome cafual blaft excites a conflagration, and the whole explodes. Even *Blackftone*, allows there are cafes when *the nation has very juftifiably rifen*. But the refentment of an injured people, in this northern climate, however ultimately decifive; has at all times appeared to be tardive, and met the derifion of thofe who were doomed to be its object. The favourites of monarchs, confided in the power of their mafters, without once recollecting, that it failed at the fame moment it became neceffary to their own prefervation. The Penfioned Conftellation * of party literature, in the fame work where he goes out of his way to call *Hampden the Zealot of Rebellion*; remarks the infenfibility of *James* the Second's courtiers to the dangers of the precipice they ftood on. What could appear more hopelefs than the Revolution, when *another Zealot of Rebellion*, the gallant *Ruffel*, lamented its impoffibility, *becaufe we had no great men left*. Yet even his father lived to witnefs it; lived to fee the weak monarch taught, that

* Viz. *Urfa major*.
† See Lord *Ruffel's* Speech on his Trial.

royalty

royalty in such hands, is but the gilded weather-
cock that tops the structure of the state. A
storm rends its sides, an earthquake roots up
the foundation, and the atom perishes unen-
quired for in the ruin. A blast too impotent
to shake the walls, may overset the bauble, and
leave the fabric unimpaired; to stand the wonder of succeeding ages, with the illustrious dignified names of *Brunswick*, or *Nassau*. Thus may
it long continue, spite of the machinations of
those who would destroy its symmetry, and
have dismembered its domain, flattering themselves that while they can drown the voice of
justice, its hand can never reach them; or con-
fiding in the idea that this country, however
irritated, can make no exertions, *because we
have no great men left*, as if, even admitting it
to be true, great events would not produce
such. From what nest of fanatics, sprang the
infant *Cromwell?* where slumbered the immortal *Washington*, till oppression called him forth
the Saviour of his country.

Whatever may be the tenets of the court on
these prints, it seems beyond he trackless chaos

of

of political cafuiftry, to frame one plaufible objection againft arming every inhabitant of a free country, and training him with all necef-fary attention. An army fuperior by its num-bers, infinitely fo by its conftituents, to what-ever the combined navies of *Europe* could land in this ifland, might be formed without ex-pence; and which, excepting the article of drefs, might in one fummer confefs no inferi-ority to any opponents. If this be really an inferiority or not, I fhall leave to the difcuf-fion of modern difciplinarians, and army taylors, who all are equal to it. Whether a man fights beft in a red coat, or a carter's frock; a flouched hat, or fool's cap and feathers, are difquifitions too nice, to be rafhly entered upon.—But if the yeomanry, the farmers, the hufbandmen of the country; together with the tradefmen and mechanics of great towns, were trained to the ufeful parts of a foldier's employ, which af-ter all, contains nothing myfterious or intri-cate; our troops might extend their conquefts on every fide of the globe, and this nation re-main in perfect fecurity, competent to its own defence.—Train them to martial exercifes, and

every

every village, whofe defiles offered a *Thermo-pylæ* could furnifh a *Leonidas*; for the rudeft ploughman in an *Englifh* cottage, wants nothing but the habitude of arms, to be formidable in ufing them. Courage forms a great part of the education of our lower ranks, and of all the qualities of the mind, none is more artificial.—In thofe of more elevated ftations, it affumes another name; and although a different texture of nerves, or degree of activity, may produce different modifications of it; yet every man of honour has precifely the fame fund of courage at the bottom, whether it be foberly confined, or fretting out at the bung-hole.—The defence of one's country is however one of the few general lights in which it can be fairly compared or reafoned upon.— An artificial production muft depend upon that fcience, addrefs and practice which have created it. From thefe alone a man derives confidence in every fituation. A fox-hunter will leap a precipice, a failor brave a tempeft that would difmay an *Ajax*. *Cæfar* himfelf was timid in a carriage, and regularly obferved

a fua fuperftitious ceremony to avert his danger when he mounted one.

The hiftory of almoft every nation abounds with inftances of fignal good effects derived from the provident exertions of individuals; and fatal evils arifing from their ignorance or inactivity. The inroads of the *Scots* formerly kept our northern frontiers conftantly arrayed, and trained to arms in the fchool of neceffity. A danger lefs immediate, frequently expofed the coafts oppofite *France* to be caught unprepared; and whenever that happened they became the victims of their own imprudence. While the fuccefs which never failed to reward the forefight of their more alert neighbours, muft have convicted themfelves, and fhould remain a monument of wifdom to their pofterity.

Stowe mentions particularly an Abbot of *Battle* in *Richard the Second*'s time, who twice preferved the town of *Winchelfea* from French depredations; whilft the inhabitants of *Rye*, " *in confidence of ftrength*," expofed themfelves to a defeat, which occafioned their town and its beautiful church to be reduced to afhes and

R   only

only eight of themfelves left alive to witnefs
it.—The conduct of this gallant Abbot is the
more meritorious, when after evincing his
courage by volunteering dangers which his profeffion exempted him from, he had good fenfe
enough to reftrain that courage from urging
him beyond the limits of defenfive war. Thus
when the enemy wearied out by his diligence,
at their fecond vifit had in vain endeavoured
by all means to bring him to action, they at
length fent to him, " requefting that if hee
" woulde not have peace, he would fend forth
" to fighte man, to man; or more in number
" if hee woulde to trie the matter in viewe of
" armes, but neithere woulde the Abbot admitte
" the one requefte or the othere, faying hee
" was a religious man, and therefore not to
" admitte fuch petition, and that hee came not
" thither to fighte but to defend, and preferve
" the peace of the countrie."——Had the *Ifle
of Wight* men been equally wife, they would
not have loft their ifland as they did about
this time, by fuffering the enemy to land, on
purpofe to give him battle.

The

The nation who in times of danger has nothing to depend on but a ftanding army is in a fituation to be pitied; but, if this country, all powerful in refources, neglecting them, fhould look up to an army that hardly exifts, the moft humane fpectator, even if too benevolent to laugh at our abfurdity would at leaft difpenfe with any tribute of compaffion.

The advantages which arife from pre-eftablifhed order imprefs themfelves forcibly upon our reafon in every tranfaction liable to buftle and confufion; thefe advantages it is vain to expect in the tumult of action. To be ferviceable then, men muft have their leffon at hand. A wife minifter can in all ages and all governments find means to form affociations, and make fervice palatable, when fuch plans do not originate in the people themfelves; *Robertfon*, in fpeaking of *Cardinal Ximenes* fays, " As " mercenary ftanding armies were unknown " under the feudal government, and would " have been odious to a martial and generous " people, he iffued a proclamation, command- " ing every city in *Caftile* to enrole a certain

R 2   " number

" number of its burgeffes in order that they
" might be trained to the ufe of arms on *Sun-*
" *days and hollidays*; he engaged to provide
" officers to command them at the public ex-
" pence, and as an encouragement to the pri-
" vate men, promifed them an exemption from
" all taxes and impofitions.—"

Not only every appeal to the fenfes and underftanding fhould be made in favour of this meafure,
but there are periods, when government fhould
fubftantiate rewards; although penalties fhould
rarely be inflicted on thofe who witheld their
fervice. Every philofophic principle of legiflature, convinces us that rewards, if not equally
powerful, are a much nobler fpring of action,
than punifhments; and as thefe have only the
negative effect to deter from evil, they muft be
mifplaced, when the active virtues are to be
roufed that impel to good. Confidered however in fome points of view, all local gratifi-
cations, partake of the nature of punifhments
operating over a certain circle, wherein they
tend either to increafe difparity of condition
already obnoxious, or to create it.

However

However education may humanize the mind, there exifts in every breaft an innate love of equality, which it never fees violated with fatisfaction. Good breeding, and good fenfe; but conceal or moderate its effects; for the beft heart, howevever fincerely it rejoice at the fuccefs of thofe in remote ranks, either above him·or beneath, withólds its delight at the luck which immediately conftitutes a fuperior of· an equal,—Fortunately for human nature, vanity fteps in and extends the line which levels our philantrophy. Some intrinfic perfection, fome peculiar quality fteals us a few inches above ourfelves, and fcftens the harfh deformity of every ftep into an imperceptible flope. My title confoles me for *Burke*'s virtue ; my próperty outbalances *Charles Fox*'s genius ; and *Keppel* with all his country's wifhes wants my conftitution. In fhort, if comforts of every other kind are denied, the redundancy of mental qualifications will compenfate for all defects. Here the Gods have been profufe in univerfal liberality. Want of health, figure, or fortune are frequent fubjects of repining ; education is fometimes blamed, but no man ever ferioufly

complained

complained of the fhallownefs of his capacity, or impeached the juftice of Providence for giving his neighbour a larger fhare of intellect. —It feems, as if not light itfelf could be more plentifully or more equally beftowed. The *tree of knowledge* grows in every hedge, and an *Agrarian Law* divides the realms of fcience to the perfect fatisfaction of every individual. *Rochefoucault,* who looked through human nature with a penetration unblunted by the affectation of common-place benevolence, painted what he faw in vivid tints, without the varnifh of flattery, and obferves that " *in the adverfity, even of our beft friends, we always find fomething to confole ourfelves* ;"—at leaft it is certain, that no man is completely miferable for any misfortunes but his own.

With regard therefore to affociators, the rewards of thofe who affembled, might be indirectly, penal upon non-conformifts, by half-rating the firft to the revenue in fome inftance, as *Roman Catholics* are doubled. A parifh ftill raifing its quota, the refidue muft of courfe fall on the others.—Or, it not being poffible

to forefee how few or how numerous the dif-
fentients would be in particular diftricts, the
feffions might be furnifhed with a general
power of relieving from highway duty, and
faddling it on thofe who refufed their fervices
to the public in another line.

A variety of fuch inducements might be held
out, which need not be recapitulated, for
thank heaven, we have a miniftry who underftand the management of douceurs.—Nor do
fuch details, conftitute any part of an author's
bufinefs, whofe authority is ineffectal towards
putting them in practice. It is fufficient to repeat, that the inhabitants of a county liable to
invafion, fhould not be unprepared for defence.
The modes of compelling, or what is much
better, of perfuading them to acquire the requifite preliminary expertnefs, are almoft infinite in the hands of legiflature. The tafk, is
fo far from being arduous or impracticable,
that a thoufand plans might be formed, for
carrying it into execution; and that fo effectually, that it fhould be a difgrace to a young
man, to have miffed the meeting of his com-
rades

rades. Government might fell them arms; to be paid for by a pound rate; a tax fo confonant to public weal, would hardly be complained of, when our patient endurance fubmits to fo many of another ftamp. The day of exercife leaft inconvenient to the parties, and beft afforded by an impoverifhed nation, would be Sunday; efpecially as the arming in defence of our religion, muft be deemed no equivocal demonftration of it; provided our pulpits inculcated it as earneftly as in the time of Queen *Elizabeth.*

To load with dexterity, to fire with precifion, to advance and retreat with order, and celerity; the habitude of deriving mutual fupport, and unity of force, from maintaining a rank, is all that need be learned, and may be acquired in very fmall detachments.—But if time allowed, the purfuing it through higher gradations of utility; when it became, as it foon would, matter of emulative recreation. The villages of a rape might meet each other during the fummer months, and on thofe days, be inftructed in the general outline of irregu-

lar

lar defence, as far as related to throwing up
flight works, or fecuring themfelves behind
walls, banks, rivulets, and abbatis.—If for
this purpofe, fome worthy worn-out officer
were called with a decent allowance, from
penury, and half-pay; it might not be the
moft exceptionable charge of the army extra-
ordinaries.

The greateft difficulty that occurs in calling
forth the fervice of mixed and large bodies of
people, is to avoid confufion; while a diftinct
eftablifhment of regularity is the firft ftep to
fuccefsful operation. Men muft not only know
the fignals which are to call them out, but
where they are to affemble, for what purpofe,
and the arms or tools neceffary to effect it.
The moft minute detail of arrangement muft
not be omitted: for the coaft, on which an
enemy attempts to land, will fully need the exertions of all its inhabitants, without a moment
to fpare, in debating how they fhould be employed. When their labours ought to have
already commenced, it is too late to plan them.
Country gentlemen cannot be expected to pof-

S   fefs

fefs the knowledge requifite for general operation.—Here government fhould take the lead.
Engineers of capacity, fhould be employed to
make accurate furveys on the coafts, the rivers,
fords, heights, roads, and defiles; with the
fituation of the villages, and number of inhabitants. Thefe fhould all be derived from
actual obfervation, a fmall diftrict, not exceeding twenty miles allotted to each, and reports
given in, after a refidence of three or four
months. Wherever Perfons properly qualified
for this employment could be procured on the
fpot, their information would probably be the
moft fatisfactory. The emoluments for this
fhould be fmall, to prevent it becoming a job,
and that no diftinction of parties might have
a chance of fuperfeding abilities. Thefe reports, would be only a foundation for the
Commander in Chief to work upon; whofe
labour being fhortened by inftructions where
to feek the important pofts, fhould vifit them
perfonally, eftablifh the fituation of beacons,
and trace out the whole plan of defence.—It
fhould be obferved that hundreds are but an
inconvenient divifion for any but civil purpofes,

it

it would therefore be better if each county were allotted into military diftricts, whofe forces might be more concentrated; each of thefe to elect fome magiftrate, or other intelligent perfon, to whom government might communicate the refult of their enquiries and deliberations fo far as was proper for his guidance. There appears no neceffity for conveying the whole of thefe in the nature of pofitive regulations, but partly as matters of inftruction *. For if it be recommended to break down fuch a bridge, make an abbatis here, or a fort there, thefe are points, which in the moment of peril will never be contefted through caprice or felf-conceit. Nothing but a certainty of better meafures from unforefeen circumftances can occafion their being fet afide; and no peremptory decifion at a diftance fhould anticipate what events may alter the nature of.

The care of the ftate fhould farther extend to the fupplying fuch cannon, arms and ftores, as their reports evinced the propriety of

* Not Law like, but lovingly.——Lord North's letter, 1587. See chap. iii. *ante*

grant-

granting; and henceforward the charge devolves upon the magiftrate or deputy lieutenant above-mentioned, who fhould lofe no time in arranging matters with the neighbouring gentlemen, and form committees to fuper-intend the regular trainings, with the addition of tracing a few flight works on the ground pointed out, wherever it could be effected,

Perhaps there yet remains fomething to be guarded againft, wherein this army of a few villages may require the interference of legiflation. No man is fo loft to all the generofity of juftice, which the gallant fentiments of this nation demand, as to fufpect any *Englifhman* would be backward in his country's caufe, if ever the hour of trial fhould arrive; few perhaps are impreffed with a contrary peril from excefs of virtue, and how probable it is for an ebullition of valour to arm every peafant with gun or pitch-fork, without order, without fyftem : and totally neglectful of thofe advantages which were immediately attainable. It fhould therefore be rendered highly penal in cafe of an actual landing or attempt to land, for any individual

dividual to difobey the orders of fuch magiftrate, always underftanding this to extend only
to his temporary command, 'till the lord
lieutenant or other fuperior legally authorifed
fhould arrive.——Secure however of this authority when requifite, all details might be previoufly arranged ; and thofe inhabitants named
who fhould repair with tools to the appointed
rendezvous, for the purpofe of throwing up
the firft work which had been already traced
before them. It fhould alfo be fpecified who
fhould fire the beacons *, who ride to array
the neighbouring villages, and quicken their
operations, which are equally methodized.——

* In order that the commanding officer at any camp or
poft with which the beacons communicate, may be able
to afcertain from what part of the coaft the alarm is firft
given, certain diftinguifhing fignals fhould be fixed on ;
for example, from the *Ifle* of *Thanet* to the *South Foreland*,
one rocket ; from *South Foreland* to *Dungenefs*, two ditto ;
from *Dungenefs* to *Beachy*, three ditto ; from *Beachy* to
Brightelmftone, four ; from *Brightelmftone* to *Selfey*, five ;
after which, to avoid confufion from a number, the
next diftrict might begin again with one rocket, being
fufficiently diftant from the firft, to obviate any miftake
from the fignals being alike. Thefe might alfo be further fubdivided, if neceffary.

Other

Other persons are previously allotted to fill trees for abbatis, and prepare fascines * ; the teams of the neareft farms to draw them. The cattle to be driven off by another fet of lefs able men, to be affifted by women and children. In fhort, every one fhould know precifely where he is to be placed, and what are the immediate fervices his country demands at his hands.

When an enemy has once obtained footing in a country, the laws which neceffity impofes upon felf-defence are dreadfully fevere; but like the operations of furgery, from fuch painful facrifices alone relief can be expected.—To confidential hands therefore muft be entrufted the cruel tafk of deftroying the fubfiftence of an enemy; frequently when danger preffes, conftrained to devote the very barns and granaries to the flames, and every where oppofed by the

---

* It is to be wifhed fome uniform ftandard adapted to military purpofes could be fettled, for tying up at leaft a part of all coppice wood near the coafts. This might be of great advantage, and the inconvenience fmall ; for fafcines, are as good as any other faggots.

plaints

plaints or curfes of the proprietor.——This
fervice however muft be qualified by the reftrictions of prudence; the enemy's fituation
pointing out the moment that muft fentence
each diftrict: left the fuperabundance of zeal
caufe unneceffary devaftition.—There are villages fheltered by rivers, woods, or moraffes
which by a little attention to guard and fortify
their bridge, avenue or caufeway, might preferve their property to the last. An open
country denies thefe advantages, and as all
forage in fuch is generally the lefs eafily procured, by fo much the urgency of having it
timely cut off is augmented.

It is not to be expected that the neighbourhood who pour in the firft day or two of a
landing, are to effect more in point of fighting
than what the mere prefence of armed men will
do; which is to keep the enemy extremely
reftlefs and unquiet, to turn out his guards all
night, and prevent his reconnoitring, fo as to
fecure important paffes before the arrival of
your army.—The impeding his route by multiplied obftacles is perfectly adapted to the

body

body thus aſſembled, and may be effected to inconquerable perfection.—Trous des loups and, fougaſſes if they have plenty of powder, are of eaſy fabric, and a few choſen markſmen in ambuſh near them would ſeldom fail diſconcerting a vanguard. Theſe are the very perfection of irregulars; they are operations attended with little hazard to themſelves, and infinite inconvenience to the enemy. An induſtrious perſevering annoyance will ſupply all deſiderata of military ſkill, and keep the invader at bay, partly by real difficulties, and partly through ignorance of what he has to cope with.

Whatever advantages this country affords which the enemy cannot ſo equally poſſeſs muſt always be attended to. Hence the introduction of fencible cavalry is judicious, in caſe a continental war ſhould call our own abroad, however ſuperfluous it may appear at preſent.—The quantity, the calibre, and eſpecially the length of artillery, are ſtill more eſſential objects. The enemy can bring none but what is of light tranſport, whereas every reſource of horſes, forage and roads is open to us and impracticable

ble for him, even if the difficulties of landing were furmounted.—There is however, one exception to long cannon, for whofoever unites the love of his country to intelligence in the art of gunnery will, above all things recommend the ufe of howitzer, as excelling every other piece of ordnance yet difcovered, Suppofing their fhell to act only as a ball in fome inftances, the ftroke of it is not lefs fatal than any other, and its direction infinitely more certain; but the properties of fhells are wonderfully more tremendous; for befides their actual effects the very fight of them with burning fufees rolling amongft the ranks, creates more difmay than the rapid execution of ten times as many cannon balls. Cafe fhot of any nature may be adapted to them for clofe action with prodigious fuccefs, as a pierrier their ufe in many fituations would be admirable; and with a trifling alteration in the conftruction of their carriages, they become fuperior to a fimilar mortar, and produce a greater range. Their commodious form, fmall confumption of powder, and a variety of other arguments might be alledged, all which may

T   be

be much better derived from the fountain head: meaning the corps of artillery; to whose diftin-guifhed merits, the united fuffrages of all that have feen fervice in the *Britifh* army do ample juftice.—Not even the navy of *England* pre-eminent as it fhines over every other line, can furpafs this body in well-adapted profeffional talents. Here are no idle extravagancies of attitude in toffing about a firelock; no precife unmeaning motions tempting *Jacquet Droz* to advertife a portable flugal man of clock work, that fhould perform the manual exactly in two feconds and an half, according to the ordinance. All here is reafoning and obferva-vation; philofophy lends her aid to mathema-tics, the laws of motion, the flight of found, the principles of gravitation, become the ob-jects of ferious ftudy and have the inveftigation of daily practice.—An effay on national de-fence muft lofe fight of its object, if it omitted to lament the neglect of a body fo effential to its purpofes. Reafon, experience and the prac-tice of wifer nations all revolt at their treat-ment; while common fenfe remains in painful dubiety whether it be more unjuft, or more

impolitic

impolitic to reward fuch a corps with the profpect of repeated promotions around, in which
themfelves are not included; and to obferve
that the higheft exertions (which with as laud-
able wifhes inferior officers in the army have
feldom an opportunity of equalling) leave
them, after many years invaluable fervice, junior
in rank to every man they ftarted with, whofe
better fortune placed him in a marching regiment.—However fatal this may ultimately
prove to a corps on which our conquefts and
fecurity depend, its fource is not difficult to
trace. Intereft and money being fure grounds
of promotion in the army naturally tempt men
of family thither, while the inferior diftinctions
of merit and long fervice are the only plea for
preferment in the artillery. Under fuch different patronage, the rife of each may eafily be
forefeen, but it will hardly be wife to urge the
difparity too far.

An object fo important to the military
powers of this nation is by no means a di-
greffion, and fince the fyftem of modern war
allows fuch confequence to artillery, all the

militia

militia fhould be trained to the familiar
branches of it. Nor merely for the fake of in-
forming them as militia, but in the hope that
when they are difbanded, every town may furnifh a number of men capable of working, the
guns which fhould be difperfed throughout the
kingdom. Every populous fpot near the coafts
that feems of confequence, fhould be provided
in time with a fmall train and fuitable ftores,
which it requires no multiplication of offices
to entruft in proper hands. The captain of the
neighbouring affociation, the neareft juftice of
the peace, even the churchwarden of the parifh could difcharge fuch a truft with fidelity,
for the public good.

I have in my poffeffion fome lances made for
an affociation in one of our maritime counties
about the year 1745, a fpecies of arms probably adopted from neceffity; or on falfe principles, if preferred for the purpofe of forcing
an enemy from the clifts.——It requires the
obfervation of veteran troops to difcover the
general inefficacy of fire arms, of which among
many inftances to be found, *Marfhal Saxe*
vouches

vouches for one very remarkable. It is of two *German* battalions giving a general volley at a large body of *Turkiſh* horſe, not more than forty paces diſtant and killing only thirty-two men, in conſequence of which the cavalry ruſhed upon them, and they were all cut to pieces in an inſtant.—It is univerſally allowed that not one ſhot in thirty takes place; nor can this be wondered at when we conſider that hitting the mark, which is the perfection of a ſoldier in action, conſtitutes the leaſt part of his military education.—In the ſmall number of trials, I have ſeen, very few from want of habitude attain the object even in the cool moments of exerciſe; no wonder then, ſo many ſhots are thrown away when all the paſſions are afloat.— It is not hence to be inferred that the influence of fear is by any means predominant; for it is certain that in the field it rarely occurs as a principle for individuals; although there are inſtances of momentary impreſſions, creating a general pannic amongſt the braveſt troops *.

* *Marſhal Saxe* alſo mentions an alarm ſpread through a victorious army, only by a caſual exclamation of, *We are cut off*.

A young

A young partridge fhooter miffing through the whole day, has certainly no fears about him: yet in the moment of eagernefs, nothing can bring the piece to its proper level but frequent practice, and the being long inured to its direction.

Thofe who in a feries of engagements, have experienced the comparative harmlefnefs of fmall arms, might upon occafion, ufe the pike fuccefsfully. But a body of raw peafants impreffed with murderous ideas of a gun, however they might brave the enemy on equal terms, will never be induced to hazard the firft onfet within reach of their lances. Yet perhaps, thefe ought not to be wholly exploded, on fudden emergencies in default of better array. For though inefficacious on the coafts, there are fituations in the more internal parts, where trenches might be fupported by them, joined to the fire arms with which the maritime counties, who had retired inwards, were all provided. This however, fuppofes a cafe of obftinate refiftance, which hardly even ought to happen, and alfo a deficiency of mufkets and

and bayonets, always to be preferred. Supposing government only to supply thefe for the fea ports, yet there is an eafy way of eftablifhing a ftandard of arms for the whole kingdom, adapted to the army ammunition.—And this by a heavy tax on gun barrels not made conformable to the ftandard for carrying an ounce ball. This can be no grievance, for if every *Englifhman* have a right to arms, for the defence of his own houfe, this is equal to any in other refpects, and fuperior as a branch of national defence. If qualified gentlemen chofe to indulge themfelves in other diverfions for their fport, the tax would only fall upon a luxury, with the additional fatisfaction to the financier, of being affured by that very qualification, of the party's ability as well as inclination to incur it.

Whenever the invaded are driven to the neceffity of active war, it can be no other than a war of pofts. Their frequent enterprizes, may attack thofe of the enemy, but their hourly attention muft be to the defence of their own. It is needlefs to repeat that the exercifes of leifure, fhould be the rehearfals of

fervice

fervice. Regiments fhould frequently be thrown
into out-houfes, courts, orchards, church-yards,
&c. They fhould be taught to feek a breaft-
work in every bank, and a rampart in every
wall. They fhould fee at the inftant, what angles of it flanked an enemy's approach; and
what other angles, buildings, or abuttments,
prevented themfelves being enfiladed. 'If no
fuch are found, the farmers facks ready
filled as they may be, or ftuffed with earth
from his garden, from fuch a traverfe in an
inftant. The advantges of an abbatis, are
fometimes to be compleatly procured in the
fhorteft time, and there are fituations wherein
they are of effential fervice, A caufeway, a
ford, a hollow pafs, invite fuch a defence. It
is applicable to every road where the adjoining meadows are divided by ditches, as they
are near *London*, and in all low grounds; it is
ftill more fo, where the inclofures are formed
by high and woody banks, like *Devonfhire*.
No man fhould be ignorant of the ftrength
his village would acquire by cutting down a
few trees, and difperfing them if poffible, in
fome faliant angle, which he can contrive to
flank. With the habitude of feeking thefe advantages,

vantages, every cottage is a fortrefs. But place me a parade ferjeant in a hamlet with a dozen fpruce foldiers, and let them be affailed by a fuperiority of force; courage may brave the unequal combat, prudence may effect a retreat through the gardens, but wifdom would have feen how fafely the poft was to be maintained, had you ever taught it him; or inculcated, that to obftruct the enemy with the leaft hazard to the invaded, is the leading principle to defenfive war.

There is no danger of cenfurable tautology, in perpetual repititions of the neceffity of works for this purpofe. They fhould be conftructed every where, and arranged in fuch minute detail, that every village fhould know where to erect them, and on what plan, whatever fide the enemy advanced on. Thus pre-inftructed, it fhould be their care to have them ready againft the arrival of the army who were to defend them, in cafe themfelves are infufficient for the purpofe. Thefe works ought by no means to be fo refolutely maintained as to hazard the troops within, who

U   muft

muft never be expofed to be ftormed or cut
off. So long as their retreat is fafely effected,
the enemy obtains no victory, and perhaps, after
a fevere flaughter, only finds himfelf mafter
of a few hundred yards, prefenting a ftill
ftronger work before him. The precife point
of time, at which evacuation is neceffary, muft
depend on the facility of the retreat, the diftance of the next poft, and the ftrength of
that they are defending. Some are tenable
if well *fraized* or *palifadoed*, till the enemy
reach the very ditch; a paffage through the
abbatis, or more remote defence, may decide
the fate of others : but the fundamental maxim
of all is ftill the fame; to defend them only
fo long as to fecure retreat. For thefe reafons,
therefore, it fhould have been obferved, that
affociations need not abfolutely confift of men
with arms in their hands, fince a corps of artificers from every village, with hatchets, pick-
axes, and fpades, might be as ufefully employed half a mile beyond the fcene of action,
in conftructing a breaft-work for the reft.
This fort of chicanery may be extended to
the moft infurmountable degree; there are

poft

pofts which cannot be turned, and to effect
this in any cafe, the enemy, under a variety
of difadvantges, muft traverfe a larger orbit,
whilft the defenders unembarraffed, mafter of
the territory, and acquainted with its roads,.
move in the interior circle. This muft always enable them to perform their marches
with fuch fuperior rapidity, as to prefent equal
difficultes in every new line of operation to
which the invaded may be driven; befides,
that all this is effectually gaining time.—And
time, by enabling the nation to call forth its
moft diftant refources, is in itfelf an hourly
victory.

Thofe who have hitherto written on the different branches of fortification, have confidered
it abftractedly, without any relative confideration of circumftances. However bewildered
and fubdivided in detail this fcience may be,
its firft principles like that of many others,
are extremely fimple; and there is no man of
common underftanding, with as decent a fhare
of mathematics as every gentleman ought to
poffefs, but what could acquire a very compe-

tent

tent ſkill in it, more eaſily, than himſelf ex-
pects. Every ſcience, it is true, diſplays gradations of merit amongſt its profeſſors, and
our corps of engineers, are very far from the
bottom of the ſcale; ſome there are, whoſe
talents, the proudeſt diſplay of foreign ſchools;
might wiſely emulate; yet I have never happened to meet with any ſyſtem of field forti-
cation, adapted expreſsly to defenſive war; and
ſtill further, to defenſive war in *Great Britain.*
There is a captious facility in putting queſ-
tions, that might aſk if the whole buſineſs of
entrenchment, be not defenſive war, and it will
be agreed to in a large extent; but great deſiderata ſtill remain. We are taught ably to defend a poſt, teach us to defend a country;
theſe are ſurely ideas beyond bare repitition,
and multiplication. One reflection ariſes from
human nature itſelf. Men will fight on better
terms, knowing a ſecure retreat to works replete with new difficulties to the aſſailant.—
Another circumſtance ſeems to alter every eſ-
tabliſhed rule of fortification, which is, that
(excepting one poſſible caſe, the laſt works
round the capital) the troops of the country
muſt

muft never be expofed to being cut off, and therefore, the flanking fire fhould be directed to a remoter diftance than the ditch of the faliant angle. The title of *Le Cointes fcience des poftes militaire*, promifes more than it performs. *Clairac* has not an idea of it; and Capt. *Pleydell* leaves us to wifh he would enlarge his fcale.

Againft a nation properly and univerfally affociated for its defence, the fhalloweft politician of an hoftile ftate would hardly project an invafion. To level an attack immediately at the ftrongeft fide is too grofs an error for the youngeft foldier; and to land a body of troops in a country like this when arrayed, would be relinquifhing all chance of equal conflict, with a certainty of incurring every poffible military difadvantage, far from every fource of fupply for repairing the cafual loffes, or neceffary expenditure of war. Whilft the inhabitants with armies ever recruiting, refources ever fpringing, and advantages ever increafing, would acquire ftrength and confidence every hour. *Montefquieu* indeed reports a faying, that " the *Englifh* were never fo eafy to

" conquer

" conquer as at home," which he qualifies by agreeing that it only holds good in the cafe of her being exhaufted by diftant wars ; and thus far it is an oracle to warn us againft the dangers of our prefent fituation, and point out the urgency of warding the blow, to which our wild heroics in *America* have expofed us. *Great Britain,* deflitute of allies, kept at bay by her own colonies, and affailed by the moft formidable confederacy, that ever threatened her dominion, has no army to look up to. That continent wherein the active valour of a *Tarleton* has been debafed, hardly admired, never applauded * ; where *Burgoyne* with courage and with conduct was difgraced, and where ten thoufand gallant undiftinguifhed efforts have been configned to perifhable infamy. That fatal continent which not the moft delirious fallies of the *Swedifh Charles* could dream of conquering, has facrificed an army, that in

* ————————— The Toil of War,
. . . .
Which hath as oft a fland'rous Epitaph,
As Record of fair Act; nay, many time,
Doth ill deferve, by doing well : what's worfe,
Muft curt'fey at the Cenfure.   Cymbeline.

defence

defence of this nation might *have braved a world* in arms. What then remains for our fecurity but to array every citizen and defend ourfelves.——Long e'er the art of fubfidizing troops created a military fyftem ufeful to commercial ftates, which made a merchandize of fervice, the nations round bore their own arms, and a man's helmet fitted himfelf alone. Thus our anceftors were their own avengers, till civilization united to wealth, introduced a more commodious and in moft refpects a better plan; but if neceffity obliges us to revert to antique cuftoms, we fhall confole ourfelves by the recollection that fuch have been practifed with fuccefs, and need not abandon our hopes while we can ferve ourfelves.

CHAP.

CHAP. V.

On the Militia.

WHEN the abolition of the feudal tenures had difarmed the yeomanry and pea-fants, whofe vaffalage heretofore rendered them immediate foldiers at the call of their refpective lords, while thefe held their own poffeffions under the fovereign, as lord para-mount; it became neceffary to frame fome eftablifhment of troops, prepared for the in-ftantaneous defence of the realm, in cafe of fudden emergencies. But as neither the exi-gencies of the ftate, or its conftitution, required thefe to be conftantly embodied; they were only occafionally trained, and then, on max-ims of the foundeft policy, returned to their different occupations. No human inftitution could

could be more wifely planned. A body of
men, firft chofen by lot, were particularly defigned and marked out, whofe fervices in the
field the nation was entitled to exact without
delay. But this was at moft periods, a remote
confideration, while their duties as citizens
were indifpenfable, and of daily advantge to
the community. To this fyftem, under various modifications, we owe our prefent militia,
the great fterling defence of this kingdom, and
the only army its unfophifticated conftitution
could acknowledge. Whatever variations have
been introduced in partial claufes, the legiflature has never yet loft fight of the original inftitution. The inhabitants are felected by ballot. Thofe of the neighbourhood are exprefs-
ly directed to be pofted together. Qualifications too, have been uniformly infifted on for
the officers, in order to give weight, and fecurity to the eftablifhment. The executive part,
has not however kept pace with the fpirit that
enacted thefe falutary laws. The fundamental
principle of embodying the inhabitants of a
county, under the aufpices of their landlords
and neighbours, has been completely forgotten.

X   Qualifications

Qualifications have firſt been ſhamefully evaded, and then neceſſarily diſpenſed with. The ad- miſſion of ſubſtitutes, in itſelf a fair and rea- ſonable accommodation under proper reſtric- tions, has been univerſally allowed without any limitation, or regulation whatever, to the ut- ter diſgrace and diſparagement of the ſervice. Whenever the perſonal abilities, manual ſkill, or commercial connexions of an individual can, by advancing ſcience, improving manufactures, or any other mode, increaſe national wealth, or ſtrengthen natural defence more than his perſonal ſervice could effect, every idea of moral juſtice unites with political expediency, in accepting ſuch a compromiſe as ſhall be moſt beneficial to the party, as well as to the community at large. But then ſubſtitutes themſeves, ſhould invariably be procured from the ſame county; for neither the private or even the relative ſituation of any ſubject, can authoriſe an alteration that deſtroys the firſt principle of the eſtabliſhment itſelf, and inſtead of arming the moſt repectable body of the neighbourhood, furniſhes a corps of aliens to the counties they repreſent: unacquainted

with

with its defence, unconnected with its interefts, and the heavieft clog to the recruiting
that army, which an annual law, declares neceffary for the " fafety of this kingdom, the
" defence of the poffeffions of the crown of
" *Great Britain*, and the prefervation of the ·
" balance of power in *Europe* *."

Befides this, it feems that by the fpirit of
the Militia Laws, our anceftors had in view
the training by fucceffion, a much larger body
of citizens to the fcience of defenfive war,
than can poffibly be effected under their prefent
fyftem. For this reafon, among many others,
by way of prelude to perfonal fervice, it is to
be wifhed, that during the time of war, when
the militia was actually called out and embodied, it could be reduced from triennial to
annual. For although the former be a reafonable period for a peace-eftablifhment, yet it
will hardly be contended, that one year of conftant excercife, is not more than equivalent to
the thrice twenty-eight days, as well as abundantly fufficient for all the practice and infor-

* Preamble to the Mutiny Act.

mation,

mation, neceſſary to make the inhabitant uſe-
ful. At any rate, the uſage of hiring ſubſtitutes, ſhould be clogged with ſome reſtrictions;
and whenever difficulties occur, they can be
adjuſted by no mode ſo congenial to the principles of our legiſlation, as by the ſummary
verdict of a jury, before the deputy lieutenants. The rights of exemption from perſonal ſervice, pleadable in ſuch inſtances, might
be the practice of any liberal art, an exten-
ſive commerce, a beneficial manufactory, ill
health, and above all, a *jus trium liberorum :* or
ſome ſimilar indulgence, ought ſtill to be allowed in this inſtance, as in the preſent depo-
pulating period, it ſhould be in a variety of
others. There are alſo caſes, in which a liberal government might indulge inclination, in
order to obviate all impreſſions of diſguſt to a
ſervice, that ſhould be rendered pleaſant. But
then caprice is a fair ſubject for taxation. Con-
ſequently, an exemption from perſonal ſervice,
ſhould be allowed *de jure*, without any ſpecific
plea for hiring a ſubſtitute, on payment of a
fine not leſs than 20 l. or exceeding fifty, to be
aſſeſſed by the jury, according to the ability

of

of the party. Without recurring to the ac-
knowledged maxim, of suffering a partial evil
that a general good may result, in order to
palliate inconvenience, and in some cases to
sanctify oppression; it may not be difficult to
shew, that the militia, on its true constitutional
footing, is no such bugbear as to induce very
frequent appeals from the ballot. Reduced, as
it is to the footing of a regular army, it acquires inconveniencies not its own, which the
farmer, the mechanic, and even the common
husbandman must wish to obviate, before he
can readily embrace it, but these grievances,
constitute no part of the militia establishment;
on the contrary, they are inconsistent with
found policy, repugnant to the spirit of its
laws, and foreign to the genius of the consti-
tution itself. A militia-man fairly considered,
is not a soldier, either by choice or by law.
The inhabitants of a country find it necessary,
amidst the hostilities that ravage the globe, to
have some internal establishment of defence;
instead of hiring domestic or foreign troops,
a certain evil, for a precarious good: they
adopt the wiser plan of agreeing by their re-
                                  presentatives,

prefentatives, that a number from their own
body fhall be confined to this charge; and
they caft lots, to afcertain the perfons to be
arrayed, for a certain ftipulated period. But
the men thus elected, are by no reafonable
conftruction, fubject to any other covenants than
thofe of being in readinefs, and in fufficient
training, for the purpofes of national defence.
They have never embraced the profeffion of
arms, or devoted themfelves to the caprice of
reforming generals. They have abandoned no
privileges, by felling the laws of their country,
and accepting an arbitrary code in exchange.
Their difcipline, fays *Blackftone*, IS LIBERAL AND
EASY, and he thinks the articles of war an hard-
fhip on them, which taken in their extent, they
certainly are; for, granting that it may be expedient to form new regulations for every different incorporation of men, it does not therefore follow, that an involuntary and fortuitous
predicament, fhould fubject a man to the fame
penalties for failure in parade, etiqutte, or even
in fome degree, neglecting a three years charge
of a fingle ifland; as for abandoning the duties
of a profeffion, which by his own act he had
                                        devoted

devoted himfelf to for life, fubject to ftated regulations, extending to all parts of the globe, and who, at the very making this contract, had received what he chofe to imagine an equivalent.

Paffing however the articles of war, (notwithftanding the authority of a *Blackftone*, and the palpable injuftice of difproportioned or arbitrary punifhments) to avoid all experiment of innovation in the hour of peril. There are points ftill more effential, which that very peril magnifies the importance of. Too long have the maffive chains of prejudice rivetted our underftandings; we have equally loft fight of what is equitable towards others or ufeful to ourfelves; and in the exercife, the difcipline, the regulation of the militia, we have fuffered fafhion to introduce all her abfurdities, to the total fubverfion of more effential defenfive principles, and with an outrageous violation of contract, that nothing can extenuate.—It may perhaps require fome degree of military fkill, or rather an enfranchifement from military prejudice to detect the manual exercife itfelf, which

like

like the hocus-pocus of a juggler, or Mr. Bayes's plot, is merely calculated to elevate and furprife; yet however well it may ferve to fmarten, or fill up the time of a foot-foldier is worfe than abfurd when extended further.—It is not legerdemain, or teaching a man the tricks of a monkey, that can either defend his country, or annoy his enemy. All thefe cere- monial performances ought therefore to be in- ftantly exploded as fenfelefs and unmeaning; even if the right itfelf of fadling them upon the militia were enquired into, it would hard- ly bear difcuffion, unlefs they could be proved contributory to the purpofes of national de- fence, for which alone the citizens of this ftate have agreed to arm.—It is no juftification of this right to alledge that the act of Charles II. which declares the militia under the com- mand of the crown, fubmitted generally the mode of training it.—For it would be replied that it could only fubmit the training it as a militia and not as an army.—To urge ftill fur- ther a fovereign and fole power of judging what is right, would be yet more unfatisfactory. To an unbounded uncontroulable prerogative,

the

the wifdom of this nation has never annexed exiftence, and no general in fupport of this unlimitted command will venture as yet to fend a militia regiment chained on board the gallies, by way of experiment to prove rowing a part of their exercife.—The fupreme command refides ultimately here, as in every other inftance is the common fenfe of the nation, the fovereign is but the mouth-piece to declare their will, and if he perverts the employ of the militia by directing it to any other purpofes than thofe of national defence, he arrogates an authority never delegated, and rebels againft that facred fource of all power, *the majefty of the people.*

When an old officer is feen putting a militia corps through all the exhibition of a parade field day, revolted reafon enquires how many of thofe pretty ceremonies are applicable to his country's fervice, and candour itfelf but reftrains the laugh through refpect for the unpliancy of high military notions, early imbibed, and confecrated by cotemporary folly.—The greateft fkill in the fmalleft matters is, the

Y   characteriftic

characteriſtic of modern tactics. A certain *ton* and *bel uſuage* have erected a ſyſtem of which the art of reaſoning conſtitutes no part. What in the name of wonder can it ſignify whether ſuch a militia regiment ſtep off with one leg, or with the other? reſt the firelock or order it? turn to the right or left about? It were better perhaps for this country, to have them do it the way called wrong than right, provided it be equally expeditious; for the time taken up in learning theſe matters, whether one hour or one month, might be much more uſefully employed,—Inſtead of inſulting the rational faculties of country gentlemen with all the puppyiſms of parade, can no exerciſe be formed on ideas of utility, and might not a little ſhow he ſacrificed in Times like theſe, to objects of intrinſic importance. If the purpoſe of the muſket be to fire with preciſion and rapidity, might not theſe be practiſed at a target, with ſome propriety. To be well acquainted with the *forte* and *foible* of their own coaſts; to judge the natural ſtrength of poſts, and the artificial modes of augmenting it, are at leaſt as eſſential, as to have hats exactly the ſame

cock,

cock, and queus exactly the fame length. But thefe notions are a fort of herefy in tactics, where ferious debates have arifen, whether a foldier's legs ought to be all white, or all black, or half of both, although neither fignified three ftraws, or anfwered any end, except that of exciting difguft in every man of common underftanding. Such however, are at prefent, important fubjects; and a war of buttons, is carried on with more pertinacity, than any other object of the campaign.

There is a maxim, which might fafely be extended to armies in general, but is an incontrovertible *axiom* when applied to militia, this is, *That all duty fhould be carried on with the leaft poffible inconvenience, confiftent with real utility.* The mind employed in objects worthy its attention, will ever give it; but long trifled with, it retaliates, and trifles in its turn. So few ufeful points are to be obtained in a feries of modern field days, that the minute portion of ore is hardly worth refining from its quantity of drofs, nor do many poffefs the microfcopic eye required, to feek it there. When an independent

country

country gentleman, relinquiſhing his fortune and his eaſe, ſteps forth to inſpire his tenants with patriotic animation, with what ſenſations can one endure a pert adjutant from the army, whiſpering an ignoramus colonel, (who conceives diſcipline depends upon it) that Captain Such-an-one wears a ſcratch wig, when he ought to appear in a bob. In the name of wonder, cannot a plain honeſt *Engliſhman*, diſplay the ſterling energy of his character, without having it debaſed by foppery, and ſophiſticated by conceit? May not a glorious ardor impell a man to ſerve his country, although he poſſeſs no talents for the *ton*. The modiſh refinements of polite life, may not have reached the happier villages which flouriſhed under his paternal magiſtracy; or perchance, the unconquerable ſpirit of *Creſſy* and *Agincourt*, has renderd the ſtern ſoul of ſome modern *Caractacus*, impervious to their penetration. *Hampden*, and *Sidney*, were plain men, whoſe appearance, would now be as unfaſhionable as their tenets; and even *Cromwell*, no bad ſoldier in his day, would make a ſorry figure at the *Horſe Guards*. For heaven's ſake, let the prevalence of folly

model

model as it will that ftanding army, which
ftate neceffity and continental madnefs, impofes on our freedom; and if a foldier cannot
exift otherwife, at leaft let us be militia-men
without being coxcombs. — Whenever it fhall
be demonftrated that a man in a red waiftcoat
is *thereby* incapable of being equally brave
with his neighbour in a white one; it will become a national concern, and the militia muft
be worried into conformity; but until that
fhall be clearly afcertained the fting of ridicule
muft await a bigotry fo idolatrous. Happy
for this nation were it only laughable, but if
by hunting men of fenfe and confequence from
the fervice it become pernicious, the joke exifts
no longer.—A declining empire cannot afford
to facrifice ftable and conftitutional fecurity to
idle foppery and the unreal advantage of military vagaries. To conftruct redoubts, to throw
up lines, to form abbatis, and defend pofts
already formed, are the true employments of
fuch troops. Even fougaffes, trous de loups,
and all the variety of device which ingenious
man has invented for his own deftruction, become (to ufe a courtly phrafe,) "*The arms which*
"*God*

" *God and Nature have furnished,*" and perhaps
not worfe applied to the defence of our laws,
our liberties and our religion, than in the
attempt to deprive our children of thefe
bleffings.

Field days fhould no longer confift of a for-
mal bill of fare, divided like the acts of a play
into a regular ftring of manæuvres.—Inftead
of thefe fhould be fubftituted frequent marches,
and the reprefentation of actual war over a line
of country; rehearfing as much as could be
forefeen on the very fpots moft liable to be the
fcenes of defence.—Flying camps fhould often
vifit the principal landing places, form on the
neighbouring heights, take pofts and fecure
them; in their retreat to others, explore the
fhorteft communication of bye roads, try every
ford, afcertain the poffibility of inundations,
found every morafs, and know the extent of
every plain. Thefe are occupations that add
ftrength, infpire confidence, and carry conviction.—To break up roads effectually, and
with expedition; to fcour the country in detached parties with fuch geographic knowledge

as

as always to fall back in the fhorteft line to a fupporting body, are things not to be omitted ; for although the troops of this country would be under no neceffity of feeking forage for themfelves ; yet the effectually cutting off all means of procuring it from the enemy is a moft material concern, and would now be feebly executed.—All militia ought to be light infantry, not by the fafhionalle mode of cutting off their fkirts, but by the rapidity of their movements, and the burthenfome irregularity of their attacks.—Their exercifes fhould rarely lead them to march the grand road : that cannot be miftaken, the enemy himfelf will follow it without erring ; but to know the diftance, the bearings, the ftrength of bye-ways, with the moft expeditious track to regain their own camp through a thoufand intricacies, are advantages he cannot poffefs, and we fhould not be without. Many a detachment had been fecure in gaining a poft within an hundred yards, when they were loft for want of knowing it. How many enterprifes have failed from troops miffing their way ? How many furprifes might have been effected,

that

that were never thought of through the fame
defect ? Our militia captains are all fox-hun-
ters, and well impreffed with the convenience
of knowing a country. Never did a general
revifit in peaceful hours the fcenes of his former
campaign without being ftruck with the difcovery of advantages miffed on both fides.—I
have twice feen regiments in *England* lofe
their way in fituations, that had been fatal, if
an enemy had exifted ; and if this can happen
without either the confufion of action or terrors
of defeat, how ftudioufly fhould it be guarded
againft, when thefe have a poffibility of
uniting.?

At prefent the firft drilling of a militia-
man confifts in marching flow time; a bufinefs
he need never be confined to above a week,
for ftately as it is, adding dignity to motion,
it conftitutes no part of defenfive operation.—
I remember formerly to have acquiefced in the
long continuance of this practice, from a conviction of the neceffity of fome meafured pace,
that fhould reduce the different movements of
individuals to uniform certainty ; and by uniting

ting the whole body teach it to acquire one momentum.—This seemed likely to be compassed with greater eafe and precifion, by commencing with paces more flow and ftrongly marked ; however the experience of an whole regiment marching in battalion with the utmoft exactnefs, without ever practifing the flow ftep ten days, has convinced me it is not neceffary.—If it be allowable as matter of rudiment, it fhould never be hunted down for the purpofes of parade. It certainly does fet the foldier upright, and fhew him in the handfomeft ftile, and wherever thefe are effential points, it ought to be the firft object of dicipline, but if one atom of convenience is to be facrificed, no advantages prefent themfelves to authorife it, fo long as the militia are not confidered as holliday puppets for the mob to gaze at.—On the contrary, the curved attitude, neceffary for many trades and moft operations of hufbandry, fo habituate the dorfal mufcles to inflection, that at a certain time of life it becomes as painful for thefe people to maintain an erect pofition, as it would be for a gentleman to remain long ftooping ; and that this is no trifling

Z   fling

fling inconvenience every one has experienced in a variety of exercifes.—For what purpofe then is the frame of man to be diftorted? Will he be more active, or better enabled to endure fatigue, in a diftrefsful than in a natural pofition?—To fuppofe that an attitude is eafy, becaufe it pleafes the eye of tafte, is irrational. —The flowing elegance of the *Antinous* imitated for ten minutes would be more inconvenient than the pillory. Few trivial points are more graceful than turning out the toes, yet the lectures of a public academy have very ably demonftrated this to be an unnatural diftortion, which if not early adopted muft be more than unpleafant to acquire.—Hence if caprice and fafhion are to new model our frames at any age, the iron bed of *Procruftes* may be again introduced. Or if fome future *Alexander* fhould have one fhoulder higher than the other, the modifh conformity of his courtiers, for aught we can forefee may deform the whole army; but even then I fhould vote for leaving the militia as their Creator formed them; it is not every general that is competent to mend his works.

Sup-

Suppofing the militia thus trained, to march
with order and rapidity in the pofture they
can moft eafily fupport, every unmeaning exhibition of the manual difcarded; the platoon-
exercife becomes an object of attention, conftantly to be practifed, with all the celerity
that exactitude can furnifh. In this, however,
the fpringing the ramrod fhould be avoided; it
is a motion of fignal effect on the ear as well
as on the eye, but not adequate to its purpofe.
Whoever going to fire at a mark, much more
to hazard his life upon a fhot, would load in fo
precarious, fo flovenly a ftile. Neither fhould
the motions of loading demand that exact precifion of time, neceffary in marching or manœuvres: the fize, the age, or the agility of
a man, muft create fome variance; one half
can never ram down their charge at all, if all
are expected to do it in equal time; and to
keep a part waiting for the reft, is reducing
the whole to the level of the awkardeft, at the
very moment activity is the moft defireable.
Hence the irregular or independent fire acquires
one of its advantages, its continuity and the
uncertainty it impreffes on an enemy's advance,

are

are additional ones; but perhaps the firing by platoons, or any larger divifions, would be entirely exploded, by confidering what further facrifice muft await its regular performance. Admitting that human nature, in every fituation, is capable of only a certain degree of attention, which we may exprefs numerically, by calling it equal to fix; then if one, two, or three of thefe degrees are employed in obferving to fire together, there remains fo many lefs to be exerted in levelling properly at the object; whereas in the independent firings, this alone occupies the mind. At prefent, it is greatly too much to fuppofe the attention equally divided; at leaft five fixths of it go to the word of command, while the obtaining a proper fight becomes a very inferior confideration. The militia therefore, not having to learn the knack of firing together, which a fet of *Automatons* would do infinitely better by a fingle fpring, have no occafion for wafting powder in the acquifition of ridiculous applaufe. Cartridges of this fort, fhould be referved for birthday fquibs: they fhould receive none without a ball, and with fuch they cannot practife too

often

often, fo long as the deftruction of an enemy is neceffary to conqueft, and their country's prefervation.—But on the other hand, if the powers expected to invade, are, like the *Indians*, on the firft inroads of *Chriftian* bucaneers, to be difmayed by the very found of fire-arms, let us in pity to humanity, obtain bloodlefs victories, and leave the platoon firing in the full difplay of fonorous infignificance.

Whatever is here fpoken of militia, extends no general reference to regular troops; whofe eftablifhment, whofe contract, whofe purpofes are different; but there are fome inftances, which common fenfe may poffibly apply.

A proper cloathing is neceffary to cleanli-nefs, and all its falutary confequences; it fhould be that which is moft convenient for exercife, and moft conducive to health. A light jacket is generally beft adapted to the former, a large cloak will be frequently de-firable for the latter.

A fierce-

A fierce-cocked hat, looks valiant, but poſſibly has not in itſelf the faculty of creating courage. If not, a round one is a better defence againſt the ſun and rain; a ſort of foraging cap with flaps, would anſwer both purpoſes, and be convenient to lie down in beſides.—Good ſhoes, and worſted ſtockings, or thread with worſted feet, are requiſite for frequent marches, and by keeping up the temperature of the extremeties, obviate many diſeaſes. The free uſe of the muſcles of the leg, and joints of the knee and ancle, is too eſſential to be ſacrificed to gaiters and tops, which in a greater or ſmaller degree, impede their motion. Some defence againſt cold and dirt, ſhould be procured in Winter, and againſt gravel and briars, at all ſeaſons. A kind of boot, or rather upper ſtocking, of woollen cloth, ſoft tanned leather, or canvas made tolerably looſe, ſhould be adapted to the ſeaſon. Theſe could be no obſtacle in walking, and would ſpare the eternal trouble of buttoning and cleaning the preſent cumberſome equipment.

A con-

A conftant attention to cleanlinefs fhould fuperfede all confiderations of parade, and with this view the hair might be cropped like a fchool-boys, for the moft diftant profpect of utility is not to be neglected for mere ornament, efpecially in a body with whom we have no right to play tricks for entertainment; who are devoted to purpofes too facred to be burlefqued with the impertinence of foppery. The plain rough-hewn *Englifh* peafant ought after three year's fervice to be returned unfophifticated to the plough tail, whereas now a militia education ruins every hufbandman it gets hold of. If this is not fatal to the agriculture of this country it is becaufe the enrollments of this clafs have not been very numerous; and, that they have not been fo, is the fortunate refult of another evil, the too common admiffion of fubftitutes. If a fmall proportion of hufbandmen are drawn away, it is becaufe only a fmall proportion of the nation are trained to arms. Thofe firft ballotted inftead of fuperadding the bufinefs of a militia-man to their own profeffions, relinquifh thefe and become downright foldiers. At the clofe of the war,

fo

fo few of them return to labour, that it is fortunate if we retain foreign garrifons enough to
eafe the tafk of juftice; for if marching regiments cannot provide for them; idlenefs will.
This however is a forry exchange for the community. Inftead of having at the end of feven
years, near ninety thoufand induftrious citizens
inftructed in national defence, the utmoft we
can now hope is to have thirty thoufand men
torn from us and trained to arms, at the immenfe facrifice of every other occupation.
Thefe are times in which national wealth can
hardly afford this, or national fecurity autho-
rize it. The morals of the militia (once reftored to a conftitutional footing) are a more
important object than any yet confidered; this
is a facred charge entrufted to the good faith
of the officers, their neighbours have indivi
dually claims upon the benevolence of thofe
who are to lead their children forth in a new
line, and public juftice eftablifhes this attention
as a debt, not only to the county, but to the
kingdom at large. When a regiment is to be
difbanded, it is by no means indifferent whether a well-regulated body is to be reftored

to

to fociety, or a gang of banditti turned loofe upon the neighbourhood.

To march the coaft militia out of their refpective counties is to weaken the powers of national defence; and this fo materially in every military point of view, that it is hardly poffible for the moft prudential arrangements in other refpects to counterbalance the inconveniencies of the prefent abfurd and illegal fyftem. Knowledge of the country is amongft the firft and principal advantages which troops at home poffefs over an enemy. To fhift every militia from its own coaft, and bring ftrangers as little acquainted with it as with the coafts of *Otaheite*, is an ingenious contrivance for deftroying this fuperiority, and reducing us to act upon terms equally unfavourable. 'Tis true we fhall not want guides ; nor probably will they : but the officer who can fteer for himfelf ftands on a very different footing. Suppofing it otherwife, the moft defireable cafe is, that fome perfon converfant in military matters could be found to conduct his party, and then the odds are very confiderable that he never attains the exact

A a   pofition

position suited to the intention of the officer who is to act in it. Thus like the ancient drama, wherein one of the personages enacted, what was recited by the other, the whole can never be of a piece; nor is it possible for the communication of ideas to be as perfect and distinct as their conception.

If an intimate acquaintance with the ground be advantageous, the state of its supplies in horses, forage, stores, carriages, artificers, &c. is no less so; this is only to be found at home, and those even of the next county must be deficient. The superior countenance and assistance furnished by their own militia to all provincial associations must not be forgotten; but above all the sacred ardor which a man feels for his own houshold gods. In one step further the enemy destroys the venerable cottage of his grandsire. His family already shudder at the prospect of roaming the unsheltered waste. Good heavens! if this situation could happen but once, and were confined to the feelings of a single individual, it promises more for *Britain's* safety, than every thing that can be urged for

moving

moving them. Indeed I never heard one argument for this, that was not abfurd and dif-
graceful. For if any colonel be incompetent to
training the militia properly at home, he is
certainly unfit to be entrufted with it elfewhere.

The ftation of the inland regiments ought
therefore to be the neareft coafts where it is
thought proper to place fuch a body.—Above
all things it fhould never be forgotten that the
quarters of every militia man ought to be the
neareft to his own abode confiftent with public
fafety,—It muft be confidered how foon he
may return to the duties of private life, and
how neceffary it is for him to keep up the
citizen in the foldier, which was indifputably
the conftitutional object of our anceftors.
That a man fhould be within reach of his own
little concerns, is by no means indifferent to
his country, which he may enrich as well as
defend. His farm, his hop-garden, a few
looms at home may all derive advantage from
his fuperintendance.——Let us again confider,
that the dangers to which this kingdom might
be expofed from foreign enemies, when the

influx

influx of commerce had deftroyed the univerfal array of lefs wealthy periods, firft induced
the inhabitants to agree by their reprefenta-
tives that a certain number of themfelves fhould
be trained for its defence.——To chufe thofe
perfons by lot for a ftated time was a fair and
a reafonable plan, but they were of courfe
to be fubject to the leaft poffible inconvenience confiftent with public fecurity.——
When an individual is thus compelled to a
profeffion, he has undoubted claims upon all
its fair conditions; and it is a very fair one,
that he fhould not be harraffed by any employment, fervice, or removal, not effentially conducive to the public fafety. It goes far beyond expedience and propriety; *it is the undoubted right of every maritime militia to remain
in its own county, unlefs the public danger be thereby
augmented*, which can rarely happen, except on
fuch coafts as appear otherwife defended, or
very remote from all probability of invafion;
or in cafe of actual intelligence of an enemy's
'defigns elfewhere. On the fame principle, the
militia of every inland county, has a juft claim
to be ftationed at the neareft poft. Thus befides

fides the great national benefit as a firft object; many will have the advantage of their own homes, moft of their families, friends and fortunes, together with a thoufand comforts, which they never meant to relinquifh; and which it is an unjuft, impolitic, and indecent violation of the contract, for government to deprive them of.

Nothing but a total ignorance of the wife principles of our laws, or an arbitrary perverfion of them, could have introduced the prefent unreafonable practice: our ftatutes from the very firft notice taken of the militia, are exprefs in fupport of this doctrine: and fubfequent acts have continued the fame equitable regulations, till very late periods.—The words of the act of parliament, 1ft *Ed.* III. Ch. 5. are,

" That no man be compelled to go out of
" his fhire, but where neceffity requireth, and
" and fuddain coming of ftrange enemies into
" the realm, and then it fhall be done as hath
" been ufed in times paft, for the defence of
" the

" the realm." This is confirmed by 4th of *Hen.* IV.

Charles the Second, in afferting his right of command over the militia, only claimed to move them in cafes of infurrection, rebellion, or invafion, as will appear by the following extract, 13 & 14 *Cb.* II. chap. 3.

" Which lieutenants fhall have full power
" and authority, to call together all fuch perfons
" at fuch times, and to arm and array them
" in fuch manner as is hereafter expreffed and
" declared, and to form them into companies,
" troops, and regiments : And *in cafe of in-*
" *furrection, rebellion, or invafion,* then to lead,
" conduct, and employ, or caufe to be led,
" conducted, and employed, as well within the
" faid feveral counties, cities, and places afore-
" faid, for which they fhall be commiffioned
" refpectively; as alfo into any other the
" counties and places aforefaid, for fuppreffing
" of all fuch infurrections and rebellions, and
" repelling invafions, as may happen to be,
" according as they fhall from time to time, re-
                                        " ceive

" ceive directions from his Majesty, his heirs,
" and succeffors."

The wife of every age, have agreed in own-
ing how dangerous it is, to truft even the moft
moderate man with power, and that the tempting command of it, which the extent of military difcipline affords; has been long too fatally alluring*. Thofe very perfons whofe influence and abilities fhould protect the rights
of the militia, have acquiefced in facrificing
them frequently to their own authority. A young
nobleman, called by the moft generous impulfe
to the head of a corps, overlooks in the animated
purity of his intentions, what other objects
may be devoted to making a fine regiment.
His own credit feems ftaked; his emulation
is roufed, a little vanity fpurs him on, and the
body entrufted to his charge, for purpofes that
ought to have been accomplifhed in the eafieft
manner, is harraffed through all the manœuvres

---

* C'eft une experience eternelle que tout homme qui
a du pouvoir eft porté à en abufer; Il va jufqu 'a ce
qu'il trouve des limittes.—Qui le diroit! la vertu mene
a befoin des limittes.   *Efprit des Loix.*

of

of modern tactics. One half of thefe are abfurdities when faddled upon the regulars. Nine-tenths are unconftitutionally extended to the militia; even if this proceeding did no harm, its grofs injuftice muft prevent its being treated merely as ridiculous; but when it is big with fuch fatal mifchiefs, it becomes criminal, and fhould be feverely punifhed. The moft atrocious of all treafons, is treafon againft the majefty of the people, and fuch is this. The fafety of this kingdom, can never depend upon the fooleries of the firelock, or the *puppyifms* of parade; but her danger muft be augmented by their injudicious introduction. Whoever would put a militia on the footing of a marching regiment, muft facrifice a greater object, a more ftable, a more conftitutional fecurity; and by direct confequence, whoever is defirous of promoting that equality, has views incompatible with the wellfare of his country. It might appear a ftrong affertion, to fay at once, that the militia ought not to be foldiers; yet furely the idea of armed citizens, is more facred and not lefs invincible; more endeared to the feelings of a *Briton*, and infinitely more

har-

harmonized to the principles of the conftitution.
The doctrine of Judge *Blackstone*, has already
been taken notice of, and the opinions of this
great man, when unperverted by courtly politics, were drawn from the richeft fources of
our invaluable code, and digefted by the moft
profound reflection. It is the want of that liberal and eafy fyftem he mentions, that at this
moment reduces the militia infinitely below
what it might be. Men of weight and confequence, not immediately in command, foon
ficken of a fervice replete with troublefome,
trifling, and unneceffary fatigue; hence the officers dwindle fo faft, that if it be better not to
enact laws, than to lead people into difobeying
them, the qualification claufes will want re-
pealing before next feffions. The mere life of
a foot-foldier, is naturally enough a bugbear
that deters the fons of farmers and decent
tradefmen, from perfonal fervice; and on the
prefent footing, it would be unreafonable to
compell it. But, there are modes of reftoring
it to credit; of training in the courfe of a few
years, a much larger proportion of the nation,
and thefe principally of the moft refpectable

B b   claffes,

claffes, whofe property and character would en-
noble the eftablifhment with fentiment, rivaling
what the boafted houfhold troops of *France*
could ever poffefs.

One of the firft fteps to this defireable
reform, is to fend all the militia in winter
not only to their own counties, which (except
in cafes of actual invafion elfewhere) it is
madnefs ever to remove them from; but to
their own homes. The private concerns of
every individual are objects worthy the attention of the ftate. Much of its wealth depends
upon them; and this alone according to the
prefent financial fyftem of war becomes a
part of military arrangement.—His children
too, the feeds of future armies are not to be
neglected, for if the population of this kingdom decreafe as rapidly as a late eminent
writer * conceives, every profpect of repairing
the havock is a matter of national importance.
The perfonal labours of thirty thoufand men
during five months annually are not to be
overlooked in times of poverty, any more than

* Dr. Price.

the

the additional exertions their prefence might occafion in the induftry of their families. In the pay and cloathing fomething might be faved, and if the convenience of the public be thrown into the fcale all thefe together will have weight.—The adjutant and ferjeants being in fact regulars employed to train the militia, might remain to take charge of recruits; for in order that the whole fhould on emergencies have a competent knowledge of their bufinefs, it would be neceffary to make a refervation of fuch as joined late in the Autumn ; but which might be a good deal obviated in future, if all ballots except cafual ones took place in the Spring. The moral good effects of this meafure might be traced beyond the re-uniting thofe bonds of fociety, which fhould never be diffolved, and which as well as the principles of qualification, the immortal *Montefquieu* extends to armies in general*.

* " Pour que celui qui exècute ne puiffe pas opprimer,
" il faut que les armès qu'on lui confie foient peuple,
" et ayent le même efprit que le peuple. * * * et que
" ceux que l'on employe dans l'armee, ayent affez de
" bien pour repondre de leur conduite aux autres cì-
" toyens, * * *—que les foldats habitent avec les citoyens,
" et qu'il n'y ait ni camp feparé, ni caferacs, ni place
" de guerre."

No military objection can be raifed upon
any reafonable grounds to fending men home
periodically, and the practice of the *King of·
Pruffia* with the higheft dreft troops in the
univerfe muft filence the cavils of the ignorant.—At any rate, furloughs ought in moft
occafions to be granted on the eafieft terms;
always to bufinefs, or emolument; frequently
to inclination, and even to caprice. To invite
proper perfons into the fervice, the going out
fhould be perfectly eafy; a difcharge fhould
never be a matter of difficulty, hardly even of
favour; for under certain regulations, it fhould
be a matter of right.—No one who can derive
effential advantage from quitting, fhould be
detained on finding a fubftitute. If a young
man was fure of getting off, when he could
engage a farm or fhop, he would readily ferve
'till fuch opportunities offered; and numbers
would be ready to fupply his place on fimilar
conditions. Thefe changes would not be very
frequent, but the more fo the better, for a
greater number of inhabitants would thereby
be trained to the bufinefs of defence.

The

The appointment of a fecond captain to each company would anfwer fome purpofes of accommodation, and enable country gentlemen of greater confequence to quit their homes when the period was fhort and ftated. One only of thefe to be in pay at a time, and to relieve each other every three months. A militia on this footing would fubject the officers to few inconveniencies, thofe of the firft property would be tempted to ftand forth; and even if the qualifications were doubled, enough would then be found.——Subalterns would probably be procured with equal facility, if the duty were really liberal and eafy ; fuppofing the fame indulgence propofed for the men of occafional leave of abfence to be ftill more frequently extended here. The pay would be no object to the defcription of gentlemen who would crowd in, nor would the duty of either commiffion be infupportably troublefome. On the prefent footing, a fcarcity of fubalterns may in time produce improper appointments, unlefs it be obviated.——Something like this might be done by reducing the captain's pay to eight fhillings *per diem*, augmenting the lieutenants

with

with this faving to fix fhillings and eight pence, and giving army rank to the enfigns after two years fervice ; this would induce young men of family fometimes to ferve firft here, under the eye of their friends and in the way of promotion. The engaging fuch is a defireable and conftitutional object, nor could it materially affect the regulars, which extending rank to lieutenants might do.

Since the value of money has fo much leffened its proportion to the neceflaries of life, the pay of foldiers is become a pittiance, that requires fome exertions of judgment, to regulate its œconomical expenditure ; and for the honour of humanity, there are many officers who have beftowed the moft meritorious attention on it. That a foldier fhould be well fed, well cloathed, and well lodged, are three points, which in length of fervice muft fuperfede every other. Thofe who are called out for a temporary exertion, may poffibly fhift for themfelves ; but in all permanent eftablifhments, the army in which thefe matters are beft regulated, will have fuch advantages over
that

that in which they are neglected, as nothing
can outbalance. Good order, health, and fo-
briety, the very foul of difcipline, depend upon
them. The fuperintendence of markets, and
eftablifhment of meffes are no ignoble attentions.
By the firft, a wholefome and proper diet is
felected at an attainable price; by the laft, fuel
and utenfils are faved : and, the very water that
boils the meat, converted into a nutritious
aliment. A foldier may fight fome day, he
muft eat every day; and a parade of puddings,
affords more folid advantages, than twenty of-
tentatious roll-callings, with half as much
flower wafted on the hair.

The fame fedulous regard fhould extend itfelf every where to the lodging of troops, frequently liable to be much crouded together.—
The windows of their apartments fhould be
conftantly open in the day-time.—Air, if the
firft of vital requifites is furely not the laft of
medical ones ; and indeed the greateft improvements of modern practice have their origin jn
attention to its effects ; hence the fuperior
afcendancy acquired over inflammatory com-

plaints

plaints, hence too the fmall pox which fo lately defolated Europe like a fecond plague, has loft its horrors; while youth and beauty triumph in its defeat.—In fultry weather, a free circulation is abfolutely neceffary to exiftence; putrid fevers of the moft dangerous kind are the immediate confequences of ftagnated air. In dry cold weather, however the hazards of neglecting this may be leffened, it ftill prefents advantages to the conftitution. While the atmofphere acts as a perpetual cold bath, it reftores the elaftic tone of the fibres, and repairs that debility, which unwearied relaxation would foon produce. When the rooms in which foldiers lodge are tolerably fpacious, I am no advocate for this communication with the external atmofphere in very damp weather; which in this climate produces more chronic diforders, than every other caufe united; this, however is fubject to fome regulation of feafons and fpace; for generally frefh air with all the confequences of dampnefs is lefs dangerous than a foul contaminated medium.—By means of proper covering, principally woollen, the pores may in many inftances be protected from ex-

cefs

cefs of moifture, while the lungs are better
fupplied for the purpofes of refpiration.—Cleanlinefs is amongft the principal articles of quartering foldiers, and fhould be moft feduloufly
attended to by the ferjeants and corporals, on
whom it principally depends; for officers cannot be conftantly in quarters. By frequent air-
ing and changing of bedding, fweeping or
wafhing rooms, moft cutaneous and many con-
tagious difeafes may be prevented.

To keep men wilfully out in bad weather,
who have few changes or conveniencies for reftoring falutary warmth, is equally impolitic
and inhuman. It requires no practice to endure
fnow or rain when exigencies render it neceffary;
but on the contrary frequent expofures hazard
the ftrongeft conftitution in fpight of every
effort of the will. *Julius Cæfar* himfelf would be
no more proof againft a Rheumatifm, than a
common drummer; and illnefs would as effectually difable the one as the other.——The appellation of fair-weather foldiers may be pro-
digioufly facetious; but until it fhall be fettled
that valour confifts in braving a hail ftorm,

C c   every

every good officer will avoid trifling with the health of individuals, efpecially when it is im-material to the fervice, whether the field-day commence this inftant, or to-morrow. For this reafon alfo, the Summer bufinefs fhould be car-ried on in the coolft hours, and moft airy or fhaded fituation. The exercifes of this feafon, fhould be the leaft violent; praftifing to load with expertnefs, firing at marks, and fuch like, Thofe of the Spring and Autumn, on the con-trary, fhould never confift of few movements, or be on bleak expofures; rapid marches, and the operations of field engineering, fhould at this time conftitute the principal employments. Not that pofitive reftrictions are neceffary to any feafon, but fome general outline fhould ever be preferved.

If any details attendant on the militia were to be entered into, we fhould be ftruck at firft fight, with the fhameful neglect of articles, whofe influence on natural defence, is of the firft confequence; and it would be impoffible not to remark, that much of the powder fup-plied by the ordnance is too weak to range its

ball

ball to a proper diſtance with effect ; and this
from a variety of miſmanagement in that myſte-
rious and inexplicable board.   Their flints alſo,
are ſo ſcandalouſly bad, as to be almoſt univerſally unfit for uſe; ſuch as no man would
think of riſking his diverſion upon after game,
are yet to be entruſted with the lives, liberties,
properties, perhaps the very exiſtence of this
kingdom; and this merely to anſwer the purpoſe of ſome vile job, ſince the expence of procuring the very beſt is of the moſt trifling nature.   If the fire of 20,000 men well appointed,
be ſuperior to that of 30,000 with the preſent
unſerviceable flints, (and it is at leaſt in that
proportion) it muſt follow, that the nation
which can afford to throw away one third of its
defence, has too large an army ; or, that if the
whole, may by any poſſibility be wanted, ſome
reform is neceſſary in the article that waſtes it.

Having obſerved as the moſt eſſential of all
points, that the militia ought invariably to be
ſent to their own homes in Winter, and to remain in their own counties at all times; it ſhould
be added, that flying camps enabling them to

viſit

viſit the landing-places therein, and rendering
them ſtill more perfectly maſters of its defence,
ſhould be their Summer deſtination; conſidering
always how ſoon they are to return to their
ſtations in private life ; which that they may
not be ſeduced from, or loſe ſight of, all opportunities of working at their reſpective trades
ſhould be caught at, and the implements of
them carried at the public expence, when not
too unwieldy. Every ſtimulus to induſtry
ſhould be conſtantly applied, and premiums
given to reward it. This is by no means incompatible with their martial eſtabliſhment, if
national wealth be a part of natural ſtrength,
which will hardly be denied. But military ideas
are too apt to abſorb every other conſideration
if its tendency to the ſame object be at all remote, however ultimately deciſive in effect.
The philoſopher reads with admiration of only
one army, whoſe foreſight during a tedious
ſiege, detached a part of its force for the rational purpoſe of begetting children for the
ſtate at home; and however ludicrouſly the
ſubject may now be handled, it was no con-
temptable ſtroke in the politics of war.

Upon

Upon the fame principles, an attention to the landed interefts of the nation demands that the militia encampments break up the beginning of harveft, unlefs in times of immediate danger. Their fervices then will be beneficial, and bad policy alone can make an eftablifhment burthenfome, which offers fuperior advantages by being ufeful in every fituation.—Nothing can extenuate the phyfical error of keeping them out fo late, as was done in 1778 and 1779, it is obvious how weighty and numerous the arguments are againft it, and the convenience of publicans the only one in its favour: for the probability of an enemy's chufing that time of the year for invafion has very little rational foundation,—To argue however the impoffibility of this, would be equally abfurd, the added difficulties of the feafon are not infurmountable, and the French minifters may chufe to incur them ; there is no reafoning upon the future deliberations of a cabinet, when our own has fo ftedfaftly borne witnefs to the truth of *De Wit*'s obfervation, *" that no wife " man can forefee the extent of folly."*—However, it may be afferted that no well-planned expedition

tion could take place very late with a profpect of fuccefs. Our climate itfelf would defeat it during the winter months, when joined to the fatigues and hardfhips ftrangers muft endure. The lands would afford no forage, the country no fuftenance; thus Nature herfelf is our ally.—But even allowing fome latitude to the injudicious timidity of government, if troops muft be kept together, the moft inconvenient cantonments are preferable to tents in *November*; barns, ftables, out-buildings, are always to be procured, and in the prefent ftate of commerce all the warehoufes on our coafts are not employed.

No tafk is more replete with Herculean difficulties, than that of combatting prejudices early imbibed, and there is fcarce a rank more overwhelmed with thefe, than the gentlemen of the army.—Entering young into a profeffion, to which they facrifice that very freedom, which in maturer years nothing could tempt a *Briton* to relinquifh; fortunately for their country, they imbibe new opinions with new laws, and feeing with juftice that their profeffion is the

moft

moſt honourable, eaſily conceive it the moſt
perfect.—Hence the deſpotic edict of command
bears a ſtamp of higher authority, than the ſacred mandates of the decalogue.—Subordina-
tion and eternal conſtraint become deities for
them, and relaxation the demon that rebels
againſt the heaven of diſcipline.—Such is their
religion ; and in every age, tenets early adhered
to, have effectually overpowered every effort
of the moſt nervous underſtanding. *Confucius*
worſhipped the idol of a *Paged*, as ſtedfaſtly
as the ſages of *Egypt* their monkies or their
onions ; even the moſt enlightened moderns
have been attached by this lethargy of reaſon,
and thus it is that officers from the army, endowed with matchleſs abilities and ſuperior
talents, bring the bigottry of their earlier
creed uncorrected to ſophiſticate the militia.

If therefore the gloomy hemiſphere of fact
intrude a mournful proſpect on the eye, at
leaſt we may travel the regions of imagination, where fancy's mirror can preſent a clearer
funſhine. Let us for a moment forget the perverſion of that liberal and eaſy ſyſtem eſta-
bliſhed

blifhed by our anceftors, and reftore, at leaft
in idea, a millitia formed on the broad bafis
of conftitutional right. Un-awed by military
prejudice, their difcipline fhall be the child of
reafon, not the abortion of fervility.—They fhall
be the foldiers of the people.—Receiving their
orders from the crown, they fhall feel that a
monarch's right of command, and their duty of
obedience depend on conformity to public
weal.—Referring to the origin of all power,
it will be found delegated for general good;
and an acquiefcence under it on other terms is
to abandon thofe very principles they are felected to protect. Their fovereign can only
fpeak the voice of the people, they can obey
no other, fo long as they continue the guardians
of the nation's rights, and not the flaves of
perverted authority.—The eafe of their difcipline, the utility of their employments, the
glory of the caufe would exhilerate every hour
of fervice, and fill the ranks with men of
property and fentiment.—Sentiment which the
importance of their charge, the love of thofe
laws, thofe liberties and that religion, they
were entrufted to preferve would animate to
the

the moſt enthuſiaſtic heroiſm. A filial attach-
ment to their native ſoil, will be ſublimed into
patriotic ardour, by a grateful recollection of
thoſe bleſſings which no other land beſtows.
—The peaſant in the humbleſt cottage of a
village, owns the felicity of that conſtitution,
which leaves him ſecure from oppreſſion in the
enjoyment of more undiſturbed tranquility,
than the grandee of every deſpotic government.
—Happy, thrice happy! if he feel theſe invaluable privileges enough to watch over them
with a jealous eye, convinced that whatever al-
lurements may induce the rich to relinquiſh
them, he, who ſhares no part in a ſyſtem of
plunder and corruption, obtains not the ſhadow
of an equivalent, nor can have any thing left
worth preſerving, if robbed of theſe. Even if
his own intereſts could be lulled, where is the
Briton who could baſely deſert his children's
title to inherit thoſe privileges, purchaſed with
the blood of their anceſtors, and confided to
his arm to be tranſmitted down with undimi-
niſhed luſtre. And ſhould a period arrive,
which heaven avert! when this glorious fabric
becomes endangered, either by the depravity

D d   of

of domeſtic miniſters, or the invaſion of foreign enemies ; there is virtue enough in this king-dom to avenge itſelf moſt amply.—Every inha-bitant would fly to arms, and in ſuch a cauſe the weakeſt becomes invincible. There was an energy in the ſouls of thoſe who graſped *Magna Charta* from the hands of a tyrant, that ſtill flows in the veins of their progeny ; and even if the ſtroke were levelled too ſuddenly to rouſe the nation at large, the militia glory to exiſt for its protection, and will ſtand forth the great bulwark of their country's freedom.

F I N I S.

APPEN-

A P P E N D I X.

COTTON. MSS. Julius, C. iv.

A. x. *Edw.* III.

Proclamacio quod quilibet armis muniatur.

16 *Febr.* Quia ex nonullorum relationibus regi eſt intimatum, quod quidam homines de Scotia quaſdam allegationes, &c. ut ſupra.. Rex mandavit ſingulis vicecomites per Angliam quod publice proclamari faciant quòd omnes homines inter etates lx. & xvi. annorum exiſtentes. Ac omnes alii homines tam milites quam armigeri, ad pugnandam potentes ſub pœna forfituræ vitæ & membrorum, terrarum, tenementorum, bonorum & catallorum. ac omnium quæ regi forſitaſſe poterunt, armis com-

peten-

petentibus, juxta formam ſtatuti apud Winton. editam, ſe muniant abſque dilatatione quacunque. Itaque quod ipſi ſic muniti ſint parati ad proficiendum pro defenſione regni, et expugnandum omnes illos qui idem regnum per terram vel per mare aut populum ſuum gravare reſumpſerint, &c. quando ex parte regis premuniti fuerint.

De ſignis faciendis.

Et mandatum eſt ſingulis ſupradiƈtis cuſtodibus portuum et littorum prædiƈtorum ſeperatim, quod aliquod commune ſignum per ignem ſuper montes, vel alio modo, in comitatibus prediƈtis fieri faciant, prout alias in hujuſmodi caſu fieri conſuevit per quod propria de periculis poterit premuniri.

Eodem modo aſſignantur ſeperatim alii homines ad arraiandum omnes homines tam milites, &c. in ſingulis comitatibus Angliæ, et ad eos ducendos ad cuſtodes portuum et littorum eorundem. m. 24. et m. 21.

Po-

Potentes alios fubfiiterent.

Ordinatio facta per regem et concilium, de hominibus impotentibus terrarum, tenimentar. et catalla, ad valorem fupradict. habentibus, alios loco fuo muniendos juxta formam pre- dictam. Et quod omnes alii, tenementa & catalla ad valent. predict. non habentes, viz. tam foreftarii, fervientes religioforum, et alii quicunque certis minutis armaturis muniantur, &c. dorf. m. 24.

Et confimilis commiffiones diriguntur quam plurimis civitatibus et oppidis primariis regni, de hominibus in iifdem morantibus, arraiandis & armandis juxta formam fuprafcriptam. In dorfo, m. 24.

Pro hominibus in portubus regni arraiandis.

3 *Octobr.* Licet rex nuper affignaverit quof- dam fideles fuos ad arraiandum omnes homines defenfibiles in comitatu Norff. & alibi infra regnum Angliæ, & ad affidendum ad arma juxta formam ftatuti Winton. &c. pro eo ta- men

men quod alieni gentis congregato navigio regnum suum invadere nituntur. Ac propter alia nova regi delata. Rex ex abundanti mandavit majore et balivis villæ de Lyne, sub forifitura omnium quę regi forfitaffe poterunt, quod omnes homines dictæ villæ defenfibiles fine dilatione arraiari et parari faciant. Ita quod fint parati, pro defenfione villæ predictæ pro repellendis hoftibus predictis, fi illuc venerunt, &c. In dorfo, m. 9.

Eodem modo mandatum eft majoribus et balivis villarum de, &c.

De hominibus per totum regnum Angliæ arraiandis contra hoftium invafiones.

3 *Octobr.* Cum rex nuper affignaverit Jo. Segrave, G. &c. in comitatu Kantiæ, ad omnes homines ibidem corporis potentes armari faciendum, viz. 40 et 20 libras terre, vel redditus, habentes, armis competentibus et equitaturis juxta ftatum fuum, &c. et omnes alios habentes cxv. li. terre & catalla ad valentiam xl. in earum habitatione, capello, ferreo, gladius,

dius, &c. Ac jam in magno confilio regis apud
Nottingham convocato, audito rumore quod
alienigene magnum navigium fupra mare con-
gregare fecerunt, fatagentes hoftiliter invadere
regnum funm, habitaque in dicto confilio de
liberatione qualiter fufficiens poffe infra dictum
regnum citius affumi poterit & ipfum regnum
defenfari : ibidem ordinatum fuit pro poten-
tiori repulfione hoftium predictorum, ac minori
onere & gravemine populi. Quod de qualibet
villa ejufdem regni, eligantur unus, duo, tres
vel quatuor, et ultra fecundum quod ville ille
minores fint vel majores, de fortioribus et
potentioribus hominibus vellarum earundem,
qui juxta ftatus fui decentiam armis competentibus muniantur.

Eodem modo affignantur allii commiffiona-
rii in aliis comitatibus ad certos numeros,
ibidem eligend. arraiand. &c. viz.

Eborum - 4500

   In Weft Riding, 1500,
    exceptis villis de Pomfret
    & Doncafter.

        In

    In North Riding, 1500,
    exceptis villis Rippon &
    Eborum.
    In Eaft Riding, 1500,
    except. vill. Beverley.

Lanc. - 4000
Lincoln - 4000

    In partibus de Lindefey,
    1334.
    In partibus de Kefteven,
    1333, exceptis villis de
    Stamford & Grantham.
    In partibus de Holland,
    1333, excepta villa de
    Sto. Botholpho.

Nott. - 1500 exceptis villis de Notting.
    & Newarke.
Leic. - 2000 excepta villa de Leicefter.
North. - 3000 excepta villa North.
Rutt. - - 400
Cantabar. - 1500 excepta villa de Cantorberi.
Hunt. - 1500 excepta villa de Huntingdon.
Norff. - 6000 excepta villa de Norwich.
Suff. - - 2500 excepta villa de Scto. Ed-
    mundo.

          Effex

Effex - - 3000 excepta villa de Colceftr.

Hertf. - 1000 excepta villa de S. Albano.

Bucks. - 1500 excepta villa de Buck.

Bedd. - - 1500 excepta villa de Bedford.

Oxon. - 1500 excepta villa de Oxfon.

Berks. - 1000 excepta villa de Reding.

Warr. - 1500 excepta villa de Warr.

Staff. - - 2000 excepta villa de Stafford.

Salopp. - 2000 excepta villa de Salop.

Wigorn. - 1500 excepta villa de Wigorn.

Glouc. - 2500 exceptis villis de Glouc. &
Briftowe.

Heref. - 2000 excepta villa de Hereford.

Suffex. - 2000 excepta villa de Cicefter.

Surr. - - 1000 excepta villa de Guilford.

Southn. - 1500 exceptis villis de Southt. &
Winton.

Somerfet - 3000

Dorfet - 1500

Devon. - 5000 excepta civit. Exon.

Cornub. - 4000

Midd. - - 400

Wilts. - - 2400 excepta civit. Sarum.

F e   Con-

Confimile in civitat. & burgis regni.

Cum in magno confilio regis apud Nottingh. convocato, audito rumore quod alienigene magnum navigium, &c. ut fupra ordinatum fuerit; quod &c. ut fupra. Rex volens concordiam predictam efficacem, forteri mandavit majori & balivis civitatis Cantuar. quod centum homines de civitate et fuburbiis eligant & armis muniri faciant, &c. Ita quod arraiata et munita uno ftandardo, pro eis ordinato prompti fint et parati ad proficiendum, &c. cum victualibus pro tribus feptamenis, &c, ut fupra.

Et mandatum eft omnibus & fingulis comitibus, baronibus, militibus, miniftris & aliis fidelibus regis ad periculis ponderatis, & confiderato quod primogenitores fui reges Angliæ in turbaciones inter ipfos & alios ex terrarum terrarum dominos motis. Domini maris & tranfmarini paffagii totis temporibus retractis extiterunt, et quod plurimum ipfum lederet, fi honor fuus regius fuis temporibus in aliquo lederetur. Quodque ipfi & ceteri homines de

regno

regno fuo pro defenfione ejufdem, fe & fua contra hoftium invafiones exponere tenentur. Prefatis archiepifcopo, epifcopo, &c. in predicto tractatu intendentes fint & obfequentes. Et poteftas conceffa eft prefato archiep. &c, caftigandum et puniendum rebelles, &c. m. 3.

HARLEAN MS. 168, p. 132.

Letters to the lord lieutenants and commiffioners for the mufters in the feveral counties hereunder named that are to fend fupplies to the maritime counties.

1599. Your lordfhips fhall underftand that her majefty hath lately received divers and fundrie advertifements, that the king of Spain doth renew his operations by fea, and doth add to his other forces of fhipping a number of gallies, and are either already arrived or very fhortly to arrive at the haven of Breft in Brittanye, which is an evident argument that he hath a purpofe to make fome attempt on fome part of the coaft of this realm, and therefore her majeftie, in her princely wifdom

E e 2 and

and provident care for the defence of this her.
kingdom and loving fubjects, doth forfee by
timely provifion to withftand and prevent his
malicious attempts ; for which purpofe we have
written our letters to the maritime counties
to have their forces of horfe and foot in a rea-.
dinefs, and we are alfo to put you in mind of
thefe fpecial directions you have received from
us by her majefty's commandment, at fuch
time as the like danger was threatened and
expected thefe late years, wherein particular
directions were fet down in what fort your
lordfhip was to govern yourfelf; and to direct
the forces of that county of A. upon notice
given you from the lieutenants and commiffioners of mufters for the counties of Devon,
Dorfet and Southampton, in fending 2000 men
into either county, that you fhall be required
upon appearance and intended courfe of the
enemy difcovered to land in either of thofe
counties, to whom befides the forefaid number
of foot, you are to fend alfo all the horfes
that are inrolled in that county, or fo many as
fhall be required of you with fuch other neceffary provifion. as by our former direction hath

been

been prefcribed unto you, whereunto we do refer you and fpecially require of you for the furtherance of her majefties fervice to perufe diligently our former directions and inftructions given you in that behalf, that there may no default be found in you in thefe occafions, concerning the defence of the realm, and withftanding the attempts of the enemy. So we bid you farewell.

Wilts, to fend	2000	to	{	Devon, Dorfet, or Somerfet.
Somerfet ——	4000	—	{	Devon, Dorfet.
Berks ——	3000	—		Southampton,
Suffex ——	4000	—	{	Southampton, Kent.
Surrey, ——	3000	—	{	Southampton, Kent.
London, ——	3000	—	{	Kent, Suffex.
Harteford——	{	1000		Effex,
		500		Suffolk.

Cam-

Cambridge	——	500	{ Suffolk,
			Norfolk.
Huntingdon	{	500	Suffolk,
		500	Norfolk.
Lincolnshire	——	3000	Norfolk.

HARLEIAN MS. 168, p. 137, b.

A letter from the lords of the council to the Earl of Pembroke, requiring him to fee the horfe and foot to be in readinefs within the Principality of Wales, and alfo to take order that the beacons be duly watched.

1599. Whereas her majeftie hath of late received divers and fundrie advertifements, that the king of Spain maketh great preparations by fea, both of fhips and gallies, with purpofe and intent to invade fome part of this realm, as we have written our letter by her majefties exprefs commandment both to the maritime and fundry inland counties of the realm, to have all the horfe and foot in readinefs to withftand the attempt of the enemy, with direction how the maritime counties fhall

be

be fupplied out of other counties adjoining as occafion fhall require. So we have thought good likewife to give your lordfhip notice thereof. And do pray you to caufe all the numbers of horfe and foot within the feveral counties in the principality of Wales (efpecialy in the maritime counties) to be likewife in rea-dinefs, as hath been in former times, and to fee the beacons duly and carefully watched alongeft the fea coaft, and meete places near the fea cofte, better to difcover any attempt, navie, or number of fhips that may come to-wards any part of that coaft, and to take fpecial regard of Milford Haven, to which end you fhall give directions that one of the deputy-lieutenants may be there in perfon, wherein praying your good lordfhippe to take prefent order: we bid, &c.

HAR-

HARLEAN MSS. 168. p. 146, b.

A letter to the Lord Cobham, Lieutenant of the
county of Kent, requiring him to take order for
the making of trenches upon thofe places where
the enemy is likelies to land.

1599. Her Majefty by advice that comes
from fundry parts finding the intelligence your
lordfhip hath heard of the Spanifh preparations
to be confirmed, and that it is greatly fufpected
by the manner of their preparations, that cor-
refpondence is held with his forces of the Low
Countries, and by advertifements and other
reafons, that he will attempt to land his forces
either in the Downes, or at Margett; her majefties pleafure is, your lordfhip fhall prefently
fend to Sir Thomas Wilford, being one of the
deputy lieutenants for the Eaft part, and to
command him forthwith to confider where
and how fome provifion may be made by cafting up trenches, or any other way of impeachment, at their likeft landing places, either in
the Downes or at Margett, which may ferve
alfo

alfo for defence of thofe forces which fhall be ufed againft them, the performance whereof we pray your lordfhip to leave to his confideration, fo it be done with all expedition; and further as we doubt not but your lordfhip will have all the foot companies in readinefs, fo befides your ordinary horfe bands we pray your lordfhip to forefee that the number of horfes may be increafed, by moving the gentlemen to bring as many of their fervants well horfed to fuch place of rendezvous as fhall be appointed. And thus, &c.

HARLEAN. MSS. 5844. p. 55.

Memorial of inftructions for fuch martial men, as fhall be employed into the maritime coafts.

For the better defence of the maritime counties, and avoyding of confufion, upon any attempt to be made by the enemy. It is neceffary to make choice of martial men, having fkill in fortification and martial affairs, to be fent down to conferr with the lieutenants or deputy lieutenants upon the points following, and to make report unto his majeftie or the

lords

lords of the councell, how they find the counties furnifhed, and put in order for defence.

Firft, it is neceffary to view the places of defcent, and to confider what fconces or other kind of defences may be made to impeach the enemy, and how fuch field-pieces as may be in the county already, or to be fent down, or furnifhed by the country, may be employed for impeaching of the faid defcent.

They having viewed the trained bands fhall moove the lieutenants or deputies, to appoint fome of the beft bands that have the moft fkilful leaders, to make head to the enemy upon any fuch defcent, and fhall alfo inftruct them how and in what fort they fhall make head, and how they fhall make retreat, in cafe the enemy fhall fet foot on land.

They fhall alfo, having viewed the ground neare to the place of defcent, make choice of fit places to retreat, to be re-inforced by pioners, whilft the trayned bands be employed in impeaching the defcent of the enemy,

where

where it fhall be meete to place fome part of
the ftrength of the body of the fhire to make
head againft the enemy.

They fhall alfo confider how the horfemen
of the county may be employed to the beft
purpofe to annoy the enemy. And therefore it
is meete they fhould be very well trayned ; to
which purpofe they are to be advifed to make
choice of fome men of fkill, to traine them out
of hand, and commandment to be given to
the lieutenants, that fuch as are bound to find
horfes or geldings, during thefe times of danger, keep them in the ftable.

That the lieutenants hazard not to fight with
the enemy, otherwife than to impeach their
defcent, until they receive direction from his
majefty, or the lords of the councell how to
govern themfelves. And therefore fome fecond place of retreat is to be thought on, in
cafe the firft fhall be forced by the enemy.

To re-inforce the places of retreat, and for
other good purpofes to annoy and impeach the

F f 2   enemy

enemy, the proportion of 100 pyoneers to every 1000 foldiers, is to be obferved. And they are alfo to be reduced under captains, and every pioneer to be furnifhed with a fkull and a black bill. To be captain of the pioneers, the high conftable will be the fitteft man, having fome fpecial gentleman appointed to be their collonell.

Places of affembly to be appointed near to the places of defcent, whereunto upon the firing of any beacon, the trayned bands and other forces of the fhire might repair. As alfo the pioneers ,to be ready at hand to be employed according to fuch plotts as fhall be fett down by the faid martial men, upon conference with the lieutenants. To which end they are before-hand prefently to take an exact furvey of all grounds and paffages, that with fmall labour and induftry may be made of ufe to ftop the enemy. And in this cafe, if the numbers of pyoneers proportioned fhall not be fufficient for the work, that the countrie, being thereunto required by the lord lieutenants or deputy

lieu-

lieutenants, fend in as many others furnifhed, as fhall be poffible.

That none fhall repaire to the places of affembly, but fuch as by the lieutenants fhall be appointed; and therefore it will be fit, that in all great towns, thoroughfares, and bridges, certain ftanding watches be appointed to examine all paffengers, and to fuffer none to pafs, but fuch as are of the known bands, and fuch as fhall have certain fpecial marks to be agreed on by the lieutenants, whereby it may appear that they be of the number that fhould repair to the faid places of affembly.

And for the better execution hereof, it fhall be neceffary that fome difcreet gentleman dwel-ling near the faid thoroughfares and paffages, be appointed to have the overfight of the faid ftanding watches, who are to have an eye to perfons doubtfull, leaft they be employed by ill-affected fubjeĉts towards the enemy.

The

The lieutenants according to former direction, to appoint captains to the reft of the fhire befides the trayned bands, who are alfo to be exercifed with fuch arms as are to be found, and muft be moved to provide drumms and enfigns, which will be fome terror to the [enemy, when he fhall fee the troops which are to make head againft him are put in fome martial order.

The captains of the trayned bands men would be perfuaded to entertayn fome fkilful lieutenants and farjeants, the charge whereof would be defrayed upon fome public contribution; wherein the recufants who do not anfwer to his majefty, the penalty appointed by the ftatute, would not be forgotten.

Some fkilful men in matters of fortification would be procured from the Low Countries for directing the pyoneers, and diftributed in the maritime counties to be ufed in cafe of neceffity.

That as well the bands of pyoneers as foldiers have a proportion of victuals for ✳ days, and

and carriages appointed for conveying the fame from place to place. For execution thereof fome fpecial perfons would be appointed to have the charge and overfight hereof.

Some carriages to be appointed for mattocks, fhovells, pick-axes, and other like tools meete for pyoneers ; and becaufe it will be neceffary befides pyoneers to ufe divers artificers, as fmiths, carpenters, and wheelwrights, it is meete that in every band of pyoneers, fome fuch artificers be placed.

That competent forces be affigned for defence of the coaft of Effex. And that befides the defence already made for Harwich, there be muftered and enrolled 200 able men out of the towns next adjoining, befides the proper forces of that place, to repair thither upon in hours warning for defence of the fame, untill the greater forces appointed thither may come. The faid 200 men to be armed and fedd by the town, and conducted by fome felected perfons.

That

That to such principal commanders, as shall be sent into the maritime counties, certain experienced captains be adjoined, to the number of 8 or 10, to each principal commander.

HARLEAN MS. 6844. p. 58.

MINUTES OF COUNCIL, 1558.

Letter to the Lord Mayor to enquire and certifie what store of powder remains in the hands of particular persons within the city of London.

The directions to the maritime counties, for withstanding the landing of an enemy. and what assistance shall be sent to their succours from the adjoining counties, to be resolved on, that letters may be prepared.

The return of the certificates of the trayned bands in all counties to be hastened for the perfecting of this proposition.

To

To confider what experienced perfons fhall be fent, to view the 'places of defcent, and have the conduct and ordering of fuch forces, as fhall be affigned for defence of thofe places.

Orders to be given for the commiffion, touching maintenance of ftallions and mares for breed, and gelding for fervice.

L. Ruffel's propofitions touching horfe in Devonfhire to be confidered.

Propofitions in 1588, *over and above thofe things in which there is order now given.*

To fee how the forces who are to repair to the places of defcent for withftanding the landing of the enemy, may be covered from the fhot of the enemy with trenches or pa-rapetts.

To make ditches and pitts where the land-ing is eafy.

To

To plant sharp stakes deep in the ground.

To have some field pieces and munition with victuals and carriages.

The horses to be kept in the stable.

And besides the horse that are reduced into band, to have the horses of the gentlemen with their retinue in readiness.

The horse as well as the arms of the recusants, to be sequestred into the hands of persons well affected.

Upon firing of the beacons. to beware of confused repair to the sea coasts, but to places of rendezvous

None to stirr but the appointed numbers without direction.

Strong watches to be placed and kept at all bridges, passages and thoroughfares.

Turn-

Turnpikes to be set up in such places.

The captains of the trayned companies not to be absent.

To know what martial experienced men are in the several counties,

It was also propounded that private captains should have under their command only one sort of weapon.

An

An * Abstract of the Certificates returned from the Lieutenants of the able, trained, and furnished men, in the several counties upon letters from the Lords, reduced into bands under captains, and how they were suited with weapons, in April, Ann. Dom. 1588.

County of SUSSEX.	Men.		Corf.	Bows.	Bills.	
Sir Thomas Palmer -	334 {	100 Cal. 60 Muf. 60	100	30	44	
Thomas Leukenor - -	167 {	60 30 60	50	15	22	
Thomas Stanny - -	167 {	30 60	50	15	22	
Thomas Bishopp - -	167 {	30 60	50	15	22	Calivers 300
Henry Shelley - -	167 {	60 30	50	15	22	Musk. 600
Nicholas Parker - -	167 {	60 30	50	15	22	Corf. 600 Bows 180

	Trained, 2004						Bills
							264
							2004
John Lonford - - -	167	{ 60 / 30 }	50	15	22	
John Culpepper - -	167	{ 60 / 30 }	50	15	22	
Walter Covert - -	167	{ 60 / 30 }	50	15	22	
Richard Shelley - -	167	{ 60 / 30 }	50	15	22	
Adam Ashburnham -	167	{ 60 / 30 }	50	15	22	
	2004						

Provisions
Powder - 400
Match - 100
Bullets - 480
Pioneers - 50
Carts - - 8
Nags - - 100

Able Men 7572
Suffex
furnished 4005

* I have given the first county exactly as in the original, to shew the form in which they are preferred; but all the others are abridged, and their amount collected into one view.

County of SUSSEX, *continued.*

	Men.	Shot.	Corf.	Bows.	Bills.	
Sir Thomas Palmer -	331	{ 104 Cal. 100 Muſ.	60	20	10	682 Cal.
Thomas Leukener -	167	{ 24 20	16	83	25	237 Muſk.
Thomas Stanny - -	167	{ 23 20	25	35	25	282 Corf.
Thomas Biſhopp - -	167	{ 30 30	70	40	25	588 Bow;
Henry Shelley - -	167	{ 30 10	40	50	31	
Walter Covert - -	167	{ 30 10	30	20	12	

Untrained {

							Bills	212
Richard Shelley	- -	167	{ 01 / 05	00	60	29		2001
Nicholas Parker	- -	176	{ 90 / 40	00	60	20		
John Lonford	- - -	167	{ 40 / 20	00	60	17		
John Culpepper	- -	167	{ 58 / 10	00	100	17		
Adam Ashburnham	-	167	{ 90 / 23	01	40	13		
		2001						

Horsemen,	{ Launces	200	00	60	Captain	**
	{ Light Horfe	204	00	60	Captain	**
	{ Petronels	030			Capt. Anthony Shelley.	

An

An Abstract of the Number of every Sort of Armed Men, in the counties through the Kingdom, taken Anno 1588.

Counties.	Able Men.	Armed.	Trained.	Un-trained.	Pioneers.	Launces.	Light Horse.	Petro-nels.
Suffex	7572	4005	2004	2001	50	20	204	30
Surrey	8552	1892	1500	372	200	8	98	29
Barkshire	3120	1900	1000	900	115	10	95	2
Oxford	4504	1164		120	30	30	150	40
Gloucester	14000	4000	3000	1000	30	20	180	35
Essex	6340	4000	2000	2000	300		200	
Northampton	1240	1240	600	640	80	50	80	
Southampton		2478	806	1672	1000	20		374
Norfolk	6340	4400	2300	2100		80	82	55
Suffolk		4239	2000	2239		80	230	84
Kent	18866	7124	2958	4166	1077	70	230	
Lancashire		3359	1170			64	265	
Cheshire		2189	2189			30	50	91

County								
Lincoln	6400	2150	1500	630	630	20	50	37
Dorfet	10000	3330	1500	1800	600	23	130	22
Devonſhire	1600	6200	3660	2550	60	120	150	26
Derbyſhire	1900	1000	400	600	100	8	50	20
Stafford	1900	1000	400	600	600	8	50	
Buckingham	2850	600	600			4	96	
Cornwall	17600	3600	1500	2100	1000	50	250	60
Somerſet	12000	4000	4000	1200		15	100	10
Wiltſhire	7400	2400	1200	500		14	40	80
Cambridge	1000	1000	500		9	19	65	
Huntingdon		400	400			20	60	
Middleſex	10000	10000	5000	5000		20	60	
Hertfordſhire	3000	3000	1500	1500	200	20	60	
Nottingham	2800	1000	400	600	100	20	60	
London	17883	10000	6000	4000		20		20
Leiceſter	6400	2150	2150					20
Total of the English ſhires certified,	158367	93779	44731	35990	7133	823	2823	503

The Abstract of the numbers of every sort of Armed Men in the Marckes of Wales, and the English Shires annexed.

Counties.	Able Men.	Armed.	Trained.	Un-trained.	Pioneers.	Launces.	Light Horse.	Petro-nels.
Salop		1200	600	600	700	28	70	
Denbigh	1200	600	400	200	160		30	100
Flintshire		300	200	100	200		3	30
Caermarthen		704	300	400	300		15	10
Radnor	1500	400	200	200	100		14	
Anglesea	1120	1120			100		17	
Worcester		600	600		100	17	83	10
Montgnmery		600	300	300	50	1	19	30
Pembroke		800	800	800	396	47	351	100
		6324	3400	1900	2106	47	351	100
Sum Total	162187	105827	18147	37889	9213	870	3078	678

Hence it appears, that the numbers actually
armed at this time were 105,827. Befides the
forces upon the Borders and the forces of York-
fhire, referved to anfwer the fervices North-
ward, which were 40,000 foot and near 10,000
horfe, and fundry fhires which are not certified.
—The Marquis of Winchefter furnifhed 4037
men, and the Earl of Suffex, 2678 ;—and we
have a very numerous lift of nobility and others,
who raifed bodies at their own expence, the
numbers of which are not fpecified, only in general terms, that they amounted to *feveral
thoufands, horfe and foot.*

It is by fimilar exertions, that a fifter-king-
dom has proved competent to her own defence, and perhaps been no lefs fuccefsful in
preferving her property from foreign inroads,
than from home-born-oppreffion.—The fpirit,
the unanimity, the unconquerable ardour, which
animated the Affociators of Ireland, merited
fomething more than domeftic fecurity.—Glo-
rying

rying in the caufe of freedom, their views were enlarged beyond all partial emolument, and in the glorious fatisfaction of emancipat-, ing the commerce of their country, Public Virtue met its firft reward in the Public Good.

F I N I S.